EVEN MORE
PLAQUES
in and around
GREAT YARMOUTH
and
GORLESTON

Published by

Great Yarmouth Local History

and

Archaeological Society

2022

ISBN 9798440362437

Registered Charity No 277272

Every endeavour has been made to trace any copyright that exists on the material in this book, but often the owner of the copyright is unknown.

If the society has contravened copyright, please accept our apologies and the publisher will be happy to include a full acknowledgement in any future edition

Cover design: Alan Hunt

EVEN MORE

PLAQUES

in and around

GREAT YARMOUTH

and

GORLESTON

Great Yarmouth Local History
and Archaeological Society

Compiled

by

Great Yarmouth Local History and Archaeological Society

Editor: Paul Davies
Plaque maker: Alan Hunt

Publications by the Society

Historic Great Yarmouth
by Margaret Gooch

Graveyard Symbolism: The Churchyard and Cemeteries, Great Yarmouth
by Paul P. Davies and B. Heriz
ISBN 978-1-5272-2967-9

A Picture of Yarmouth: 200 Years of Built Heritage
ISBN 978-095769228

Annual Journals

Monographs

Monograph One:
Excerpt from the Sailor's Home Logbook 1861 to 1864

Monograph Two:
Record of the Surviving and Legible Memorial Slabs in St. Nicholas' Church, Great Yarmouth at the Commencement of the Restoration Work: 2nd June 1957

Monograph Three:
Little Yarmouth

Monograph Four:
Homocea: YH 573: A Diary of the Autumn Herring Fishing Season: 1908

Monograph Five:
Photographs of Great Yarmouth taken between 1942 and 1944

Monograph Six:
Plaques in and around Great Yarmouth and Gorleston ISBN 978-0957609204
by Alan Hunt, Margaret Gooch and Paul P. Davies

Monograph Seven:
Window Display par excellence The work of Philip Musgrave-Gray of Palmer's Department Store, Great Yarmouth in the 1930s
by David McDermott and Paul P. Davies

Monograph Eight:
A Snapshot of Great Yarmouth 150 years Ago
by Paul P. Davies

Monograph Nine:
Some Bye-Laws of Great Yarmouth Borough Council 1862-1873

Monograph Ten:
Caister Causey Act 1722

Monograph Eleven:
A Proposal for a New Cattle Market and Slaughter House for Great Yarmouth 1877

Monograph Twelve:
A Selection of the writings of Harry Beale Johnson, the Yarmouth Mercury Corner Man 1926-1932

Monograph Thirteen:
The High Stewards of Great Yarmouth

Monograph Fourteen:
Reprint of the Great Yarmouth and Gorleston Guide 1909

Monograph Fifteen:
Great Yarmouth: the mid-nineteenth century.
Illustrated by contemporary engravings by Colin Tooke

Monograph Sixteen:
Steer's Directory of Great Yarmouth 1878

Monograph Seventeen:
Rules for Housekeepers at Palmers 1884

Monograph Eighteen:
Large Scale Map of Great Yarmouth 1885

Monograph Nineteen:
Great Yarmouth 1937 to 1969: from the Great Yarmouth Mercury

Monograph Twenty:
Society Bulletins 1 to 56 (1968-1979)

Monograph Twenty-one:
Great Yarmouth 1970 to 1999: from the Great Yarmouth Mercury
ISBN 979-8775883713

Monographs 1, 2, 4, 5, 6, 7, 8, 9, 10, 11, 12, 13, 15

are available on-line at:

www.greatyarmouthlocalhistoryandarchaeology.com

Great Yarmouth Local History
and Archaeological Society

On 25th January 1888, the Great Yarmouth branch of the Norfolk and Norwich Archaeological Society was formed. On 27th February 1953, the Society became independent and its name was changed to the Great Yarmouth and District Archaeological Society. At the Annual General Meeting on 15th May 2009, it was decided to change the Society's name to the Great Yarmouth Local History and Archaeological Society in order to reflect members' changing interests.

The aims of the Society are: to encourage the study of history and archaeology, especially in the Great Yarmouth district; and to secure the preservation and conservation of historic buildings and monuments within the town and district.

Its activities include lectures in Christchurch, Deneside, Great Yarmouth, at 7.30pm, on the third Friday of each month, January to May and September to December. The lectures are on local and national, historical and archaeological topics.

At least two excursions are organised each summer, including a coach trip to a place of interest in East Anglia, and an evening visit to a village or a site.

The Society's journal is a compilation of articles, written mostly by local people on mainly local historical and archaeological topics, and is published each autumn.

The Society produces a quarterly newsletter, giving news, articles and notices of events, which is sent out by email or post.

The Society also erects blue plaques around the district to commemorate buildings people or events of local interest.

The Committee
2021-2022

President: Andrew Fakes

Chairman: Paul Davies

Secretary: Patricia Day

Treasurer: Christine Silver

Committee Members: Gareth Davies, Stuart Burgess, Ann Dunning, Alan Hunt, Peter Jones, John Smail, Patricia Nelson, Glen Johnson, Ben Milner

INDEX

Preface

This third book records more blue commemorative plaques, which the Great Yarmouth Local History and Archaeological Society and Gorleston-on-Sea Heritage have erected in the Borough.

Commemorative plaques are an excellent way to identify historic buildings and historical associations, which might not otherwise be evident. They appeal to people of all ages and backgrounds, both to residents and visitors alike. It is clear that in the Borough of Great Yarmouth, the blue plaques have captured the public imagination and, perhaps, have increased local pride.

In 1866, London's blue plaques' scheme was commenced and it is one of the oldest of its kind in the world. There are now around 850 plaques in London, whereas Great Yarmouth and district now has over one hundred (June 2022). Since 1986, the London blue plaques scheme has been administered by English Heritage. However, English Heritage does not erect plaques outside Greater London, hence the need for local societies throughout the country to administer their own schemes and there are now several in operation in England.

The Great Yarmouth Local History and Archaeological Society's blue plaque scheme was commenced in 1981, with a plaque erected on St Peter's Plain to commemorate the Zeppelin raid on the town in 1915. After a hiatus of some years the number of plaques erected has risen, particularly over the last ten years. Such is the interest in the scheme that recently the Borough Council Conservation Department, local individuals and local businesses have come forward to sponsor the cost, for which the Society is very grateful, as their funds are limited.

The Society has chosen a royal blue background with white lettering for its plaques and tries to maintain a uniform font. The plaques are now made of aluminium composite material, suitable for external use. Other possible materials include ceramic, stone, slate, steel, bronze, brass and cast iron, but most appear to have a limited life-span and are expensive.

During 2011, the Society replaced the first plaque, which had deteriorated and had been in place for 30 years. It is hoped that the newer di-bond material will last even longer. However, we have to contend with sunlight and seaside atmospheric conditions.

Before a plaque is erected, many factors have to be taken into account. These include: the person, event or building must deserve recognition; the owner of the building must give consent; if the building is listed or in a conservation area, planning consent may be necessary; the position of the plaque must be such that it does not adversely affect the appearance of the building; the plaque must be visible from a public right of way; and it must not be in a position where it could be easily damaged.

The Society is grateful for the help given by many people and organisations over the years. These include: BBC Radio Norfolk and Anglia News; the sponsors of plaques; the *Yarmouth Mercury*; the unveilers, particularly the Mayors of Great Yarmouth; Society members; and Alan Hunt, who has made and erected many of the plaques.

The members of the Great Yarmouth Local History and Archaeological Society are to be congratulated on the erection of so many blue plaques and it is hoped they will continue with the scheme for many years.

Paul P. Davies

Victims from the Battle of Waterloo

The Great Hospital (former Royal Naval Hospital), Queen's Road, Great Yarmouth
Unveiled and sponsored by the Mayor, Shirley Weymouth
21st October 2015

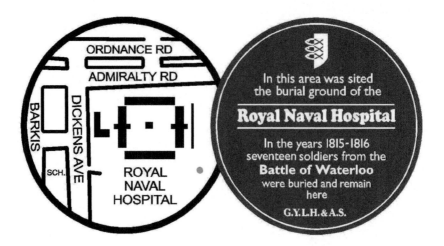

By the time the Great Yarmouth Royal Naval Hospital was built in1811, the war at sea with France was over, and it was not required for sick or wounded naval personnel. Therefore, on the 28th July 1814 the Royal Navy relinquished the hospital to the army and 600 victims from the Battle of Waterloo were sent in 1815 and they, as the records state: *were very comfortably provided for.* There is also a record dated 13th July 1815. *Transported from Ostend, 300 sick and wounded soldiers removed in keels to the hospital on the Denes*; that being the Royal Naval Hospital.

Royal Naval Hospital

In 1979, during the excavations for a new ward (the Mountbatten Ward) in the southeast corner of the hospital site, two adult skeletons were discovered about three feet below ground level. They were thought to be about 150 years old. The possibility of a plague pit or cholera burial ground (the last major epidemic was in 1849) was discounted because of the siting of the graves in relation to the town wall and the orderly arrangement of the skeletons. A painted wooden board recorded burials recorded in the south-east corner of the hospital. This stated: *in commemoration of one sergeant of the 55th Regiment, seven sailors and seventeen Waterloo soldiers who were interred in this burial ground during the years 1815 and 1816 and several children. Nomen et Arma Locum Tenent.* The Latin translates as: *their reputation and achievements are commemorated here.*

Archaeological studies suggested that this was probably the burial site for the hospital, because of variations in soil colour at regular intervals. The remains were both male and between 25 and 35 years of age. There was evidence that they had been buried in thin-walled coffins. Eleven days later, on the 29th November 1979, a further two skeletons

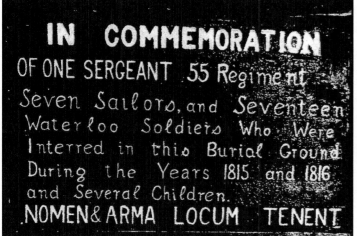

were unearthed. There is no evidence in the hospital chapel's archives that the southeast corner of the   site was used as a burial ground. The skeletons were reburied on the site in a service conducted by the hospital chaplain and the other two were left in situ. The burial plot in the hospital grounds was used from 1811 to 1816. However, there was no evidence in the hospital chapel's archives that the southeast corner of the hospital site was consecrated ground.

Paul P. Davies

Gorleston Jubilee Cottage Hospital

High Street, Gorleston
Introduced by Les Cockrill.
Unveiled and sponsored by Councillor Babs Wright for Gorleston-on-Sea Heritage
7th August 2015

This was the first hospital in Gorleston other than anything that may have been offered by the Gorleston Priory. It came about at the instigation and through the persistence of Mr Harvey Harvey-George, Manager of the Hewett Short Blue fishing fleet. Mr Harvey-George spoke on several occasions of the urgent needs of men coming ashore having been injured often days ago with the nearest hospital being rather inaccessible in Great Yarmouth. He also made the point relating to the aged and infirm that they could not afford to travel to Great Yarmouth nor could they readily walk from the tram stop to the hospital.

In December 1886, Messrs. H. Harvey-George and A. W. Blake held a meeting in St. Andrew's Hall, Gorleston, to consider a Fishermen's and General Hospital for Gorleston; Mr Harvey-George

The first cottage hospital, Gorleston

suggested that it could also celebrate Queen Victoria's Golden Jubilee (1887).

Meetings, chaired by Harvey-George, were held to progress this matter. On 4th February 1888, it was agreed to rent Mr. Brand's house, now 235 High Street, also known as St. Andrew's House, for one year as a suitable place for the hospital. On 25th February, the committee appointed Dr. Meadows as a governor, a matron at £35 p.a. including lighting, coal and dress, but excluding board and Mr. Hindle, of the High Street, as a dispenser at £10 p.a. By 10th March, the committee were purchasing bedding from G. B. Palmer and furniture from Mr. Howlett.

The Gorleston Jubilee Cottage Hospital was officially opened by Harvey Harvey-George on 26th March 1888. The ceremony was preceded by lunch at his house for about 30 people.

There was a psalm and prayers at the opening and in the evening there was a concert in St. Andrew's Hall in aid of hospital funds.

By 28th March, the hospital was in business. It had several rooms and two beds. As well as a matron, there was a night nurse, cook and general assistant. However, in April there was an appeal to complete the hospital's furnishing.

The hospital reported a level of use of which these statistics are an example: April: 12 outpatients and one admission; May: 44 outpatients and one admission; June: 33 outpatients, one admission and one infant died of influenza. A report on the first three months since opening stated that the hospital had dealt with 90 outpatients of whom 17 were the result of accidents; three inpatients were admitted of whom two were discharged cured and one was remaining, but doing well. The hospital also was doing well with many visitors and gifts from local dignitaries, including one pound from the Duke of Norfolk. In August, the Friendly Societies' Demonstration, a parade from the Tramway Hotel through the High Street to the Congregational Church, clad in full regalia and headed by the band of the Royal Naval Artillery Volunteers followed by a service conducted by Rev. E. Hall, raised thee pounds ten shillings for the hospital.

However, the hospital was encountering some problems; with two beds in the only ward so that the hospital could not admit men and women at the same time and the stairs were presenting difficulties. Additionally, the nurse caught typhoid fever, that was attributed by some, to the poor sanitation and poor air circulation. The expenses for the first nine months of operation included four pounds five shillings for keeping the nurse whilst she was ill with fever, which Harvey-George hoped would not occur again. On 7th September 1888, the governors were discussing the offers of land north of the recently extended Trafalgar Road (East) to be gifted from the Surbiton Lodge grounds by Harvey-George and the plans for a purpose-built cottage hospital prepared by Mr. H. D. Arnott.

That same month, September 1888, the matron reported on the first six months of the hospital's work, including a tally of 164 outpatients and, that there had been no inpatient admissions during September, because both beds were occupied. In November 1888, the hospital received gifts from the Harvest Thanksgiving Service held at St. George's Chapel and gifts of money, equipment and flowers from many sources. Reports of the hospital being busy with outpatients and a few inpatients continued in the local press through to at least the end of November 1889. These references include an inquest held at the Cottage Hospital on 3rd March 1889 on George Dunn aged 16 years of 20 Trueman Terrace, High Street, who drowned at sea: and the death at the Cottage Hospital on 28th April 1889 of Samuel Warner Durrell aged 61 years. As the cottage hospital in Trafalgar Road was still at the plans and contract stage, this must refer to the Jubilee Cottage Hospital.

At a public meeting at St. Andrew's Hall, in December 1888, concerning the building of a new cottage hospital, Mr. Harvey-George thanked those, who had been working at the existing hospital for the last nine months. The nine month statistics were nine admissions, of which seven had recovered, the other two were still in hospital and there had been 224 outpatients treated. That, he considered, showed how an institution of that kind was needed in Gorleston and did not mean to compete with Great Yarmouth Hospital.

The cottage hospital in Trafalgar Road East was officially opened on 29th August 1889 and it would seem that the use of the building, that is now 235 High Street, tailed off over the next three or four months. It probably returned to use as a private house early in 1890.

Les Cockrill

The Armoury (Arsenal, Barracks)

Southtown Road, Great Yarmouth
Introduced by Paul P. Davies
Unveiled and by the Mayor, Councillor Malcolm Bird
14th June 2016

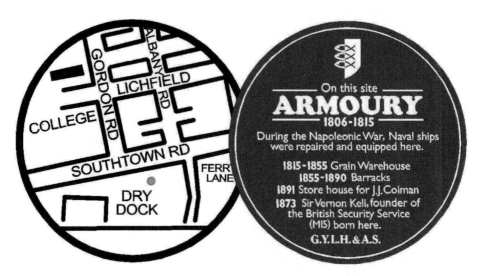

On this site
ARMOURY
1806-1815
During the Napoleonic War, Naval ships
were repaired and equipped here.

1815-1855 Grain Warehouse
1855-1890 Barracks
1891 Store house for J.J.Colman
1873 Sir Vernon Kell, founder of
the British Security Service
(MI5) born here.
G.Y.L.H.&A.S.

The lodges, barrack block, armoury and workshop survive from the original Board of Ordnance store of 1806-1815. It was designed by James Wyatt (1746-1813).

The armoury was built to serve the naval fleet anchored in Yarmouth Roads during the Napoleonic War (1793-1815). There were parallel ranges of storehouses extending westwards from a quay on the River Yare to enclose a working area, which included a small magazine. In 1806, the armoury was built at a cost of £15,000. During the Napoleonic War, 10,000 weapons were stored at the armoury for

The Armoury

the troops. It could also equip two ships of the line, four frigates and six sloops and carry out repairs to ships damaged in battle. Great Yarmouth was chosen for the site of such an establishment as Denmark had become an ally of France and it was important to stop the Danish fleet combining with the French fleet.

At the end of the Napoleonic War in 1815 the Government no longer required the armoury. In 1819, the weapons were sent to the Tower of London and the stores to Woolwich. The establishment was broken up and the premises were let as warehousing for grain and other uses. However, for most of the time it was not utilised. In October 1855, the Lichfield Estate offered the freehold of 197 acres in Southtown, which included wharves, warehouses, many dwelling houses, cottages and rich marsh land. Included in the sale was the armoury of three acres, two roods and 33 perches. *The premises were described as follows: It has the very considerable frontage on the east to the river and is bounded by the capital Turnpike Road from London to Yarmouth. The property consists of very substantial buildings, known as the Armoury, on lease to the Government, all having good frontage with sufficient depth of water for vessels of heavy burden.*

However, with the outbreak of war with Russia (Crimea War) in 1855 the armoury was converted into a barracks. Mr. W. England, a gentleman, was instructed by the Government to make the Armoury ready for the reception of the Militia Artillery. He had received from Mr. Robert Fenn, the storehouses and buildings. These premises had previously been in the possession of Mr. Watling, who used the buildings as granaries.

By the end of December 1855, the Norfolk Artillery had occupied the newly created barracks. Three regiments of Irish Militia subsequently occupied the barracks in succession (the Fermanagh, the Louth and the Donegal Militia). After peace with Russia the Norfolk Artillery Militia and the East Norfolk Regiment of Militia resided at the barracks. They were followed by troops of the line.

The officers' quarters were in houses with gardens fronting Southtown Road. One of these house was occupied by the ordnance storekeeper. There was a hospital in the barracks and, during the year 1878, 74 troops were admitted to the hospital. The average annual number of the men in the barracks was 121 and the average number of daily sick was 3.37. In 1878, at a medical inspection of the hospital it was stated that it formed the north part of the barrack square. Candles and oil lamps supplied light. As to the barracks; the latrines and urinals were flushed daily and emptied into the river at low water. The ash pits were also emptied daily. The officers' latrines were on a cesspit system and lime was used as a disinfectant. Bedding was a straw palliasse, two blankets, one rug and two sheets. An extra blanket was available in severe weather.

Armoury site in the middle ground from the air

When the military withdrew from the premises in 1889, the property was put up for auction, but received no bids and was withdrawn. By 1890, the Armoury had been condemned as being unfit for habitation and in 1891 J. & J. Colman of Norwich purchased the site. They had also acquired the warehouses adjoining the barracks. The site was used for the storage of rice and grain for the manufacture of mustard at their Norwich factory.

In 1941, the site alongside the river was considerably damaged in bombing raids during the Second World War. After the Second World War the premises were used for offices and light engineering work. Today (2016) the premises are occupied by Atlantic Marine and Aviation (on the site that was bombed), Abbey Chemicals and Elm Contracts.

In 1982, a cannon (of the Armstrong pattern) dating to the mid-18th century was discovered by the brick gate pillar of the premises. On 25th February 1982 it was unearthed by the Great Yarmouth Archaeological Society and placed on a replica carriage outside the Fisherman's Hospital in the Market Place, but moved a few years ago to the Quay opposite the Town Hall. A further cannon was unearthed in 2014.

Demolished buildings on the site include two parallel ranges of storehouses, which ran from the east side of the Armoury to the riverside. They were built to a common plan: each storehouse was a single-storey building of 15 bays divided into stores of 5 bays. The rear walls of these stores formed the perimeter wall of the site.

Adjacent to the Armoury was a magazine, which was built to an adapted version of the standard Board of Ordnance Magazine plan, but was half the length (35 feet as opposed to 64 feet). Other buildings which no longer remain include the officers' quarters, stable, chaise house and fire engine house, all of which occupied a single-storeyed building on the south site of the site, west of the armoury. The property is Grade II listed.

Paul P. Davies

Major-General Sir Vernon George Waldegrave Kell KCMG., KBE., CB
Founder of M15

The Armoury, Southtown Road, Great Yarmouth
Introduced by Paul P. Davies
Unveiled and by the Mayor, Councillor Malcolm Bird
14th June 2016

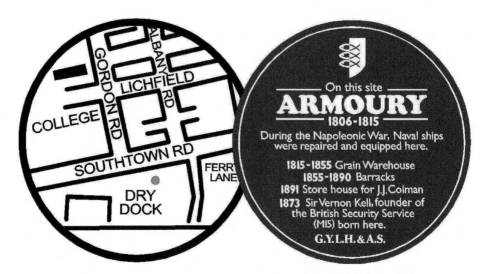

On this site
ARMOURY
1806-1815
During the Napoleonic War, Naval ships
were repaired and equipped here.

1815-1855 Grain Warehouse
1855-1890 Barracks
1891 Store house for J.J.Colman
1873 Sir Vernon Kell, founder of
the British Security Service
(MI5) born here.
G.Y.L.H.&A.S.

Vernon Kell was born in the Armoury, Southtown Road on 21st November 1873, while his father was serving as a lieutenant there. Vernon Kell was the founder and first Director General of the British Security Service (MI5). He was known as K. Kell was the son of Major Waldegrave Kell of the 38th Foot and his wife, Georgiana Augusta Konarska, the daughter of a Polish émigré, Aleksander Konarski, a surgeon with the 1st Podhalian Rifle Regiment.

Kell graduated from the Royal Military College at Sandhurst and was commissioned into the South Staffordshire Regiment in 1894 and fought in the Boxer Rebellion in China in 1896. Kell could speak German, Italian, French, Chinese, Russian and Polish. After his return to London from China in 1902, Kell was employed to analyse German intelligence at the War Office until 1906. During the time of his appointment, the Government was considering how best to fill a serious gap in the country's defence arrangements. There existed no organization to cope with the rising dangers of German espionage nor one to obtain secret intelligence on German military expansion. The Cabinet approved the creation

Vernon George Waldegrave Kell

of a Secret Service Bureau to cover these functions. At 36 years of age, in 1909, Kell was chosen as one of its first two directors and shortly afterwards took over full responsibility for the defensive side. He was chosen as his appearance did not make him look suspicious. He was to hold this position for the next 31 years and must therefore be regarded as a founding father of the organisation which later became known as MI5. The Bureau was separated in 1910 into two distinct sections and were later re-titled MI5 and MI6.

By using his instinct, observation and word-of-mouth, Kell started off with contacting chief constables and asking for information on anyone looking suspicious. Then he started a card index system. By 1914, he had gathered 16,000 pieces of information which were typed up, filed, indexed and cross-referenced. By 1914, Kell employed only three officers, one barrister, and seven clerks. Nevertheless, on the first night of the war he was able to round up a ring of 21 German spies meeting in a barber's shop in north London in an effectively timed and executed coup, which probably deprived the Germans of any information on Britain's initial military deployments. By the end of the war he had accounted for 35 more spies, some of whom were executed, to complete a wartime record, which impressed the general staff and ensured the continuance of his organisation into the peace, though on a much reduced basis from its final wartime strength of 800. During the First World War, Kell worked closely with the Special Branch of Scotland Yard and was also successful in tracing the work of Indian revolutionaries collaborating with the Germans during the war.

In December 1938, having reached retirement age, Kell asked to remain in post on a year-to-year basis. With the onset of Second World War, MI5 finally were given the hiring and financial resources of which it had been starved for years. However, MI5 proved unable to deploy them without confusion and Kell and his deputy, both in their mid-60s, got the blame. On 10th June 1940, Kell was dismissed on the instructions of Winston Churchill after 30 years in post. He then enrolled as a special constable. His wife wrote later that Kell never coped with the humiliation. He was the longest-serving head of any British Government department during the 20th century.

Kell was knighted for his services shortly before his death in 1942, was an officer of the Legion of Honour and held many foreign decorations. He reached the rank of major-general and fly-fishing was his chosen hobby. From first to last he kept himself out of the public limelight. At the end of the 1930s his health began to fail, as result of severe attacks of asthma, and he died at Olney from pneumonia, Buckinghamshire on 27th March 1942.

Sir Vernon Kell was a distinguished public servant, the longest serving head of any 20th century United Kingdom government agency or department. He was conscientious, brave, a man of high principle with a profound sense of duty, but perhaps a shade too inflexible. It is said that in the early days of the First World War he refused to attend Prime Minister Asquith's Sunday morning cabinet meeting on the grounds that he had duties to perform at his parish church in Weybridge. According to Sir Dick White (Director-General of MI5, 1953-56), Kell was *a calm, modest and patient man.... He did his considerable best in a highly demanding post during world wars, political upheavals and a rapidly changing technological landscape between 1909 and 1940.* His successes earned Kell an acknowledgement to be the best counter espionage expert in the world. He could smell a spy like a terrier smelt a rat. He practically invented the term spy catcher.

Several contemporary novelists used Kell as a model for their stories.

Paul P. Davies

HMS Lutine, the Financial Crisis and the Great Yarmouth Connection

Maritime House, Marine Parade, Great Yarmouth
(Formerly the Shipwrecked Sailors' Home)
Introduced by Paul P. Davies. Unveiled by the Mayor, Councillor Shirley Weymouth.
21st March 2016

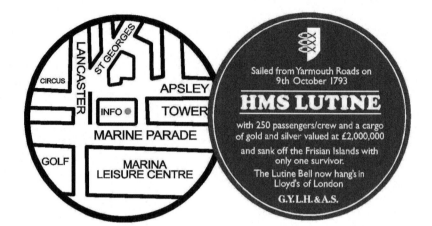

If you asked anyone to name a famous naval ship; first on the list would be the *Victory* and probably the second would be the *Lutine*.

It is not widely known that, arguably, one of the most famous shipwrecks in the world happened to a ship that sailed on its last fateful journey from Great Yarmouth. That is *HMS Lutine.*

HMS Lutine in extremis

She was built and launched by the French. The ship passed to British control and was taken into service as *HMS Lutine* and was rebuilt as a fifth-rate frigate. She sank among the West Frisian Islands during a storm in 1799.

Before the start of the Napoleonic War, communication from London to France was via Dover and the short sea route to Calais. The Post Office packet boats carried the mail not only for France, but also for Germany, Austria and Italy on this route. During the Napoleonic War it was not possible to use the Dover and Calais route because of marauding enemy ships and privateers. Therefore, the Dover packet boats were transferred to the Harwich Packet Station, whose 60-ton vessels carried the mail to the Dutch ports. Even so the crossing of the North Sea was a hazardous business. Post Office packets were official vessels and armed with 4 four-pounder guns. They relied on speed rather than their armament. Numerous accounts of the capture of the packet boats have been recorded. Because of further packet boat losses, in 1785, the Post Office was forced to transfer the Packet Station from Harwich to Great Yarmouth.

With intermittent war raging across much of Western Europe near the end of the 18th century, by about 1795, Hamburg had replaced Amsterdam as an important hub for the commodities trade. The sudden shift of activity to Hamburg was accompanied by speculation, a rise in prices, and an expansion of credit. From 1795 to 1799, Hamburg boomed. However, the summer of 1798 was dry and the autumn wheat harvest was poor. A harsh winter of 1798-99 iced over the harbour, immobilizing ships, and hampering the transfer of goods from ship to shore. As speculation further drove up prices, consumption decreased, and by spring, supply greatly outstripped demand and prices fell. Bills of exchange, which had previously expanded, now contracted, sales fell, and prices plummeted. By August 1799, the crisis had begun in earnest with Hamburg in the grips of a violent commercial downturn. As the years went by very large sums of money owed to continental merchants had built up in the City of London and it became imperative to ship the gold somehow and with the maximum amount of security. Also money was needed to be sent to the army fighting in continental Europe. Since the Post Office packets were inadequate for the purpose, the merchants sought help from the Admiralty, who agreed that a naval ship should attempt the passage. *HMS Lutine* captained by 32-year-old Lancelot Skynner R.N. was chosen.

During September 1799, convoys of wagons, with armed escorts, began to carry the gold, silver, as well as thousands of Spanish coins, in boxes to Great Yarmouth. A few days before departure, bullion to the value then of over £1,175.000 (figures vary, but it was a lot of money) was put on board the Lutine, which was anchored in the Roads. Alongside the crew there were about 30 representatives of the London Banks, travelling as passengers.

On 8th October 1799, a ball was held on board the *Lutine* with local dignitaries attending. The order to sail came during the ball and the guests were hurried ashore. She set sail for Cuxhaven (the port for Hamburg) from Yarmouth Roads in the early morning on 9th October 1799 with a fortune on board.

In the evening of 9th October 1799, during a heavy north-westerly gale, the ship having made unexpected leeway, was drawn by the tide flowing into the Waddenzee, onto a sandbank in Vlie (Fly) off the island of Terschelling in the West Frisian Islands. There, she became a total loss. All but one of her approximately 250 passengers and crew perished in the breaking seas. The gold was mainly insured by Lloyd's of London, who paid the claim in full. In 1838, the complete archive of Lloyds was destroyed by fire, so it is not possible to know the exact value of the bullion on board *HMS Lutine*. An uncorroborated newspaper report in 1869 referred to the Dutch crown jewels belonging to the Prince of Orange, which had been recently reset by those well-known London jewellers Rundell and Bridge, were on board. This was unlikely.

Over the years, many attempts have been made to salvage the bullion, but shifting sandbanks have disrupted salvage attempts and the majority of the cargo has never been recovered. The gold was apparently stored in flimsy casks bound with weak iron hoops and the silver in casks with wooden hoops. Within a year of the wreck, these casks had largely disintegrated, and the sea had started to scatter the wreck with sand covering it. Salvage attempts ceased by 1804. Over the years several other attempts were made, but very little bullion has been recovered. In 1886, a cannon was salvaged and presented by Lloyd's to Queen Victoria. It is now on display at Windsor Castle. Another cannon is on display at the Guildhall in London. More are on display in Amsterdam's Stedelijk Museum, and at least four are in Terschelling.

The ship's bell, engraved *ST. JEAN – 1779*, (St. John the Baptist under whose protection the *Lutine* was launched) was recovered on 17th July 1858. The bell was found entangled in the chains originally running from the ship's wheel to the rudder. It was re-hung from the rostrum of the Underwriting Room at Lloyd's. It weighs 48 kilograms (106 lb) and is 46 centimetres (18 in) in diameter. At Lloyd's the bell was traditionally struck when news of an overdue ship arrived; once for the loss of a ship and twice for her return.

Paul P. Davies

Site of Gorleston-on-Sea Railway Station

Station House, Lowestoft Road, Gorleston
Introduced by Les Cockrill
Unveiled by Tony Mallion, the grandson of the Gorleston signal-box attendant
Sponsored by Councillors Marlene Fairhead and Babs Wright for
Gorleston-on-Sea Heritage
19th June 2017

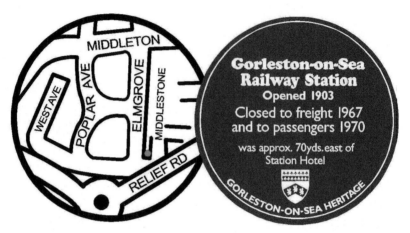

The Gorleston-on-Sea Railway Station was opened in July 1903 with, apparently, no ceremony. However, there was controversy and there were objections before work even started. The owners of property in and developers of the Cliff Park Estate plus Avondale, Clarence and Park Roads all objected to the Norfolk and Suffolk Joint Railway's plans because those roads were originally planned to have direct access onto Lowestoft Road, so not only were some property owners likely to lose land but they claimed that their properties would lose value because of the loss of direct access onto the London trunk road (Lowestoft Road).

However, permission was granted and the railway line along the coast connecting Great Yarmouth to Lowestoft was constructed. The sequence of stations, not all of them operational for the whole of the life of the line, was Great Yarmouth Southtown, Gorleston North, Gorleston-on-Sea, Gorleston Links, Hopton-on-Sea, Corton, Lowestoft North and Lowestoft

Gorleston-on-Sea railway station

Central. Many older residents of Gorleston will remember making regular use of this line to travel to either Lowestoft or Great Yarmouth at which it was, of course, possible to change to main and branch lines in order to conveniently travel to most places in Norfolk and Suffolk or direct to London Liverpool Street.

As a result of the Third Schedule of the Transport Act 1947, the London North Eastern Railway, the London, Midland and Scottish Railway, the Midland and Great Northern Joint

Great Yarmouth bound train at Gorleston-on-Sea railway station c 1937   Courtesy of Peter Jones

Railway and the Norfolk and Suffolk Joint Railway were all transferred on 1st January 1948 into the ownership of British Railways

British Railways proposed the closure of passenger services at Gorleston-on-Sea station but in response to protests reinstated a limited service. At some time in the 1960s the station was reduced from two to one operational platform.

Freight service at Gorleston-on-Sea was discontinued in July 1967, just 64 years after the station first opened, and passenger services were terminated shortly after that, in May 1970.

The site of the station is now approximately that of the major roundabout that forms the junction of the A47 dual carriageway relief road and Victoria Road.

A feature of the Gorleston-on-Sea station was the extensive goods yard and carriage sidings which, on occasion, contained the Holiday Camps Express carriages. The station was ideally situated to serve the many boarding houses and hotels at the south end of Gorleston; not least of which was The Station Hotel, now Station House.

Les Cockrill

Jem Mace (1831-1910)
Prize-fighter and World Heavyweight Boxing Champion

Hinchingbrook Restaurant, 6 Marine Parade, Great Yarmouth
Introduced by Paul P. Davies and unveiled by the Mayor, Councillor Malcolm Bird
18th October 2017

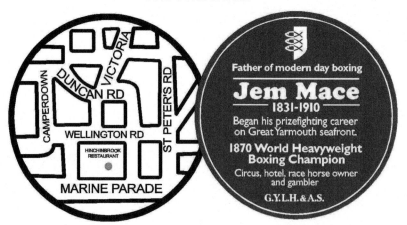

Jem (James) Mace was born on 8th April 1831 at Beeston, Norfolk, the fifth of eight children born to William Mace, a blacksmith.

A middleweight, Mace succeeded in out-boxing heavier opponents thanks to his dancing style, clever defensive tactics and powerful, accurate punching. He pioneered the left jab and worked on the art of feinting and slipping punches. He was a defensive master, but could also knock men cold with a single blow. Jem Mace brought a more scientific style of fighting to the ring than did most of his predecessors. He became known as the father of boxing and often fought boxers much heavier than himself.

Mace began fighting at 14 years of age in 1845, taking on lads from surrounding villages. He was a skilful violinist and started his working life as an apprentice cabinetmaker and as a busker. While busking outside a public house on Marine Drive in Great Yarmouth, he was set upon by four drunken fishermen, one of whom broke his violin. Mace knocked out two of the men and the other two fled. A spectator gave Mace a guinea and suggested that he became a prize-fighter (bare-knuckle fighter), thus starting his career.

Jem Mace

Before the age of 21 years, in 1850, he fought the Norwich Champion, John Pratt, losing after 69 rounds, taking just over two hours. Mace finished the fight with two broken hands. A rematch was made, but Pratt forfeited the fight for £25. However, they did meet in the same year and Mace whipped Pratt in 10 rounds lasting 30 minutes. The year later he beat the Suffolk Champion at Harleston and the Lincolnshire Bull Dog and won £10.

The prize ring was brutal in the extreme. Men smashed each other's faces to a pulp with bare fists, pickled to make them iron-hard. While boxing has always included punching, historically it also included grappling techniques like throws, arm locks, chokes as well as kicks. Punching, scratching, kicking, throwing, stomping, and strangling were all acceptable.

Prizefighting was illegal and usually took place in isolated places away from the eyes of the police. Crowds of up to 10,000 would walk long distances to see a fight. These techniques were banned during the several rule changes, which turned bare knuckle boxing, into the modern sport of boxing with the drawing up the Marquess of Queensberry Rules in the 1867.

Prize-fight

Mace defeated Slasher Slack in Norwich in 1855 in nine rounds and nineteen minutes winning £5. His success brought him to the attention of Nat Langham, an English middleweight bare-knuckle prize fighter, who hired him to man his touring boxing booth, taking on all comers for £2 a week, thus developing his skills.

In 1861, Mace agreed to fight Sam Hurst, considered the English middleweight boxing champion, by virtue of his victory over the title-claimant, Tom Paddock. Hurst, a noted wrestler, outweighed Mace by about one hundred pounds. Mace eluded Hurst's rushes and in the eighth round, knocked him unconscious. Mace was now the middleweight boxing champion of England.

As middleweight champion, Mace toured the country in a circus before facing Tom King, the heavyweight champion of England, in 1862. Mace had taken notes on King's style, an unusual practice in those days. On a cold, rainy January day, Mace struggled for 22 rounds with the larger King, who outweighed him by about 25 pounds. King's punches closed Mace's left eye and almost closed his right. In the 30th round, Mace back-heeled King, who fell on his head. In the 43rd, a left to the throat and a throw to the ground ended it for King. Mace fought over half the fight with a broken arm.

In 1869, as he was hounded by police, he moved to the United States, where prize-fighting was still flourishing and where he was just as popular as he was in England. In New Orleans he beat Tom Allen in 1870 to win the world heavyweight title.

Even within the constraints of 19th-century transport, Mace also fought in Australia, New Zealand, Canada and South Africa and was acclaimed *as the man to whom we owe the changes that have elevated the sport.*

Later, Mace continued as a purely exhibition boxer and his last recorded entry into the ring was in 1909 when he was 78 years of age. Mace was an astute businessman, who owned goldmines, circuses, racehorses, hotels and public houses, among other ventures around the world.

Mace married three times, twice bigamously. He also kept two teenage mistresses. He was a seducer of dozens of women and he fathered 14 children by five different mothers.

During his life he made and gambled away a considerable fortune. It is estimated that he earned £750,000 in his lifetime, today's equivalent of £20 million. He died on 30th November 1910, as a penniless busker in Jarrow, Durham and was buried in an unmarked grave at Anfield Cemetery in Liverpool. In 2002, the Merseyside Former Boxers' Association erected a memorial headstone by his grave.

Mace was elected to the Boxing Hall of Fame, New York in 1954. It is no exaggeration to say Mace was the Muhammad Ali of his age, the first global sporting superstar.

Paul P. Davies

Sergeant Harry Cator VC., MM., Croix de Guerre)

5 Beaconsfield Road, Great Yarmouth
Introduced by Paul P. Davies
Unveiled and by the Mayor, Councillor Malcolm Bird
14th June 2016

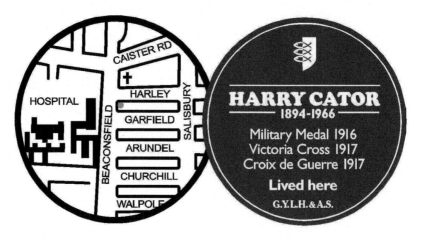

Harry Cator

Cator was a recipient of the Victoria Cross, the highest and most prestigious award for gallantry.

He was born in Drayton in Norfolk, the son of a railway worker. After leaving school, he was a porter at Beach Railway Station, Great Yarmouth, on the London Midland and Great Northern Joint Line, before joining a building contractor in Great Yarmouth. Immediately prior to joining-up to the army, he was employed by Messrs. Chateau & Co. of Southtown. Before the war he was a regular attendant at St. Paul's Church, Yarmouth and his wife was a Church District Visitor and a Sunday School Teacher.

Cator lived at 5 Beaconsfield Road in Great Yarmouth with his in-laws Mr. and Mrs. W. J. Morris. He joined the British Army in September 1914 and arrived on the Western Front in June 1915; already a sergeant in the 7th Battalion, the East Surrey Regiment.

In 1916, at the time of the Somme Offensive, he was awarded the Military Medal for bringing back 36 wounded men from no-mans land.

He earned his Victoria Cross and a Croix de Guerre first class with laurel leaves during the Arras offensive. On 9th April 1917 near Arras, Sergeant Cator's platoon had suffered heavy casualties from a hostile machine-gun. Under heavy fire Cator, with one man, advanced across the open to attack the gun and when his companion was killed, he went on alone. Picking up a Lewis gun and some ammunition drums on his way, he succeeded in reaching the enemy trench and sighting another hostile machine-gun, he killed the entire team and the officer. He held the end of the trench with such effect that a bombing squad were able to capture 100 prisoners and five machine-guns.

A few days later he was injured by an exploding shell and was repatriated to the Beaufort War Hospital in Bristol. After the war, Cator worked as a postman and as a civil servant.

Cator served with the rank of captain in the Home Guard during the Second World War and was a commandant for a prisoner-of-war camp. He retired from the Army in December 1947. He died in 7th April 1966 in Norwich and is buried in Sprowston Cemetery.

His Victoria Cross is exhibited in the Lord Ashcroft Gallery at the Imperial War Museum, London.

Sergeant Cator wrote home about mining on the Western Front: *Sounds have been heard by the sentry and mining engineers, who have listened with their instruments. Yes, the enemy is mining. So we must counter-mine. The miners start to work to try to get to the enemy as quickly as possible. This is a very dangerous task, because the enemy may have noticed your work or even heard you at work, so he stops work in his own gallery and puts a sentry to listen for you and branches off in another direction. Our miners work on, swift and silent as possible.*

But, the keen ears of the enemy sentry has heard the noise of your falling chalk as you pass to his right or left or under him or perhaps above him. The enemy engineers drive a bore through and a cylinder of poisonous gas is discharged into your gallery killing and gassing the miners. One of the preventatives for this is to take canaries down in cages, which of course, soon die at the first sign of gas, thus warning the miners. Another method of stopping your work and progress is to wait until you have passed and then put a charge of high explosive in and blow up your gallery. But, our miners are very careful and work more silently than the Boche, and more often than not he is caught. Besides, we always work much deeper, as a rule, and so foil him in this way. Then, it is a race who can get the mine in first.

Our mine is ready, the charge has been put in and stemmed. The generals know and have issued orders to certain regiments to be ready to take the outer lip of the crater caused by the explosion. The bombers are loaded with bombs, ready to leap over and take possession scarcely before the earth has had time to settle. Others are ready with picks and shovels to consolidate the position and dig communication trenches back to the front line. The men are crouching in their trenches and the mine is to go off at a certain time. The guns are going to put a barrage on the Boche's front line.

The mining officer pushes down the handle, the earth gives a terrible shudder, there is a great dull explosion and tons of earth are suddenly thrown up in the air; crash go the guns and the shrapnel comes whistling and shrieking over. The bombers are racing over the broken ground to get to the great pit just made.

Simple is the brief report, which one reads in the daily paper: 'British Official: Last night we exploded a mine under the enemy's position and occupied the crater.' But, as soon as the mine explodes the enemy's guns open fire and he also puts up bright lights, which makes the night almost as light as day. Machine guns are also crackling and he sweeps the space between the mine and the front line with deadly fire. Those working on the trench that is to connect up to the crater are put at a fearful risk. Often many are killed or wounded. The enemy also works up to the lip of the crater and tries to hurl bombs and so our bombers have to work like mad to keep him away. Your front line gets a heavy shelling, so that those carrying bombs, sandbags etc. to those in the crater also get a bad time. This is one of the minor operations that the men have to go through, working and struggling through the reek of shells all through the night.

As dawn breaks, things generally quieten down until the enemy gets his trench mortars ready. Then he trains them into the crater. It reminds one of putting a basin on a table and throwing peas into it. So, I will leave you to guess the awful time the men spend, who are detailed off to hold positions such as this.

Paul P. Davies

The First moving Pictures to be taken in East Anglia

The lookout building on the end of Gorleston Pier
Introduced by Paul Godfrey
Unveiled by the Mayor, Councillor Malcolm Bird
Sponsored by Councillor Babs Wright for Gorleston-on-Sea Heritage
17th October 2016

In the summer of 1896, two strangers to Gorleston walked along the pier and set up a tripod mounted wooden camera, and pointed it inland towards the harbour bend.

By then the locals must have been used to seeing photographers, like Alfred Yallop and James Liffen with their cumbersome mahogany and brass cameras, recording scenes and events in the neighbourhood. But on this particular day, East Anglian photographic history was about to be made.

The cameraman was Birt Acres or his assistant, Arthur Melbourne Cooper. Their camera was no ordinary one, as it took moving photographs. The camera had been made the previous year by engineer, Robert W. Paul.

It is possible that the very same camera had been used by Birt Acres to record the finish of the Epsom Derby in the summer of 1895.

Birt Acres (1854-1918)

Acres or Cooper shot the very first moving pictures to be taken in East Anglia. Their first subject was a paddle tug towing the fishing smack *Thrive* (YH 120) out of Great Yarmouth harbour. A second shot in the sequence shows the smack *I Will* (YH 723) also leaving the harbour. *Thrive* was owned by William Buckle of 67 South Quay, Yarmouth and *I Will* was owned by A. Bland of 57 St. George's Road, Yarmouth.

The film was one of 21 shown by Birt Acres on July 21st 1896 to the Royal Family. This was the day before Princess Maud married Prince Charles of Denmark. The audience enjoyed the performance so much that Acres was invited to film the wedding.

The Gorleston pier film was shown to Great Yarmouth audiences at the Royal Aquarium in March 1897 as *introducing the Cinematograph with local pictures of fishing boats leaving Yarmouth Harbour*. This was one week after the very first presentation of *living photographs* in Great Yarmouth at the Liberal Club Assembly Rooms in the Market Place.

The plaque carries information so tablet and smartphone users with access to the internet can look at the archive footage while standing where Acres or Cooper stood over 120 years ago.

The archive cinematograph footage can be viewed on:

the East Anglian Film Archive web site http://www.eafa.org.uk/catalogue/1410

or on

the British Film Institute's YouTube pages: https://www.youtube.com/watch?v=ua2MStD2J00

Paul Godfrey

The grave of Birt Acres at Walthamstow
Inscribed: A pioneer of the Cinematograph

A still from the film

John Berney Crome (1794-1842) known as Young Crome
Landscape Artist

19 King Street, Great Yarmouth
Introduced by Paul P. Davies
Unveiled by the Mayor, Councillor Malcolm Bird
12th February 2017

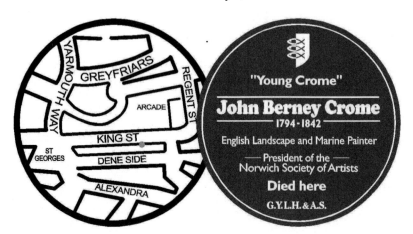

"Young Crome"
John Berney Crome
1794-1842
English Landscape and Marine Painter
—— President of the ——
Norwich Society of Artists
Died here
G.Y.L.H.&A.S.

John Berney Crome

John Berney Crome was born in Norwich, Norfolk. He was the eldest son (of two) of eight children of John Crome a distinguished landscape artist and founder of the Norwich Society (School) of Artists. John Berney Crome attended Norwich Grammar School until he was 18 years of age, where a friend and fellow pupil was George Vincent (another artist of the Norwich School). As a child, with ambitions of becoming an artist, he accompanied his father on sketching expeditions. By the age of 12 years he was painting in oils and at 16 years was sketching landscapes in water colour. A year later he was selling his paintings. It is said that he inherited the charm of his father. He was an articulate and a good speaker.

Later, Crome assisted his father in teaching, and was appointed landscape painter to the Duke of Sussex. He became a member of the Norwich Society of Artists and exhibited many of his pictures there between 1806 and 1830. He was appointed Vice President of the society in 1818 and subsequently President on several occasions, firstly, in 1819, at the age of 25 years.

On the death of his father in April 1821, Crome continued his father's art teaching practice and occupied the family house in Gildengate Street, Norwich, to which he added a studio. Now, he was probably the leading figure in the Norwich art world. In 1822, the *Norwich Mercury*, reviewing one of his paintings, felt that he promised to surpass the talents of his father. This promised was never fulfilled. In conjunction with John Sell Cotman (another Norwich School painter who for some time lived at 83 Southtown Road, Great Yarmouth; see *Plaques in and around Great Yarmouth and Gorleston,* pp104-5), Crome took a lively interest in the re-opening of the Norwich Society of Artists in 1828, which had closed in 1825 after the demolition of its old premises.

John Berney Crome had many works exhibited at the Royal Academy, the British Institution and the Society of British Artists in London. He made many trips to the continent, drawing and painting in France, Holland, Belgium and Italy. From the mid 1820's, he painted interminable moonlight scenes. His most famous painting is the Yarmouth Water Frolic, thought to have been started by his father.

Because of his extravagant habits, Crome was made bankrupt in 1831, when the contents of his father's house were sold, and many of his father's paintings and his own works were disposed of. He moved to Great Yarmouth in 1835, where he continued to teach drawing. He had health problems and, perhaps, a drink problem. He died in September 1842 at his home, 19 King Street, Great Yarmouth. After his death, the Norwich Society of Artists collapsed.

Crome was twice married, leaving a widow, but no children.

Yarmouth Water Frolic by John Berney Crome

John Berney worked in oils, water colours and pencil, painting coastal and rural scenes, both at home and abroad. His work shows the influence of his father, and he painted many moonlight effects. Many of his works can be found at the Castle Museum in Norwich.

Yarmouth Bridge 1837 by John Berney Crome

Moonlight over Breydon 1842 by John Berney Crome

The Norwich Society of Artists was started in 1803 by John Berney Crome's father, John Crome (Old Crome) (1768-1821) and his friend Robert Ladbrooke (1770-1842), as a club where local painters could meet to exchange ideas. Its members included: Henry Bright, Old and Young Crome, Joseph Stannard, James Stark, George Vincent, John Sell Colman, Thomas Lound, etc. The Norwich School's unique achievement was the production of a large body of landscape oils and watercolours, painted largely in the open air by a comparatively small group of self-taught working-class artists.

Reference:
Hemingway, Andrew, *The Norwich School of Painters*, Phaidon, Oxford, 1979

Paul P. Davies

John William Nightingale (1850-1911)
Entrepreneur and Impresario, Hotelier and Refreshment Contractor

New Beach Hotel, Marine Parade, Great Yarmouth
Introduced by Colin Tooke
Unveiled by the Mayor, Councillor Malcolm Bird
12th February 2017

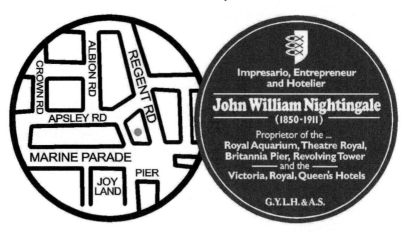

Impresario, Entrepreneur and Hotelier

John William Nightingale
(1850-1911)

Proprietor of the ...
Royal Aquarium, Theatre Royal,
Britannia Pier, Revolving Tower
—— and the ——
Victoria, Royal, Queen's Hotels

G.Y. L.H. & A.S.

Samuel Nightingale bought Shadingfield Lodge from its original owner and builder, James Cuddon, for his residence in 1873, the year after the Prince of Wales had stayed there for the first time. In the 1880s, Samuel was a magistrate and a councillor for the St. Nicholas ward. By 1887, he was the head brewer and a partner at Lacon's brewery. He continued to offer his house as accommodation for the Prince of Wales on his subsequent visits to the town.

Samuel's son, John William, left Great Yarmouth when a young man to work in London, where he gained considerable experience in the catering trade with the firm of Bertram and Roberts. He worked at the Crystal Palace, Alexandra Palace and the Westminster Aquarium. For four years he was the licensee of the Olive Branch public house in Edgware Road.

John returned to Great Yarmouth in 1882 and, the following year with a partner Mr. Pullen, he took on the lease of the refreshment department of the recently refurbished Royal

John William Nightingale

Aquarium, on the Marine Parade. Two years later, they became lessees of the whole building and were also lessees of the Marine Palace in Margate and the Aquarium in Scarborough. On 16th August 1884, Nightingale began to serve *six-penny fish dinners* at the Aquarium, following an idea he copied from the huge International Fisheries Exhibition, held in London from May to October 1883. Baroness Couttes, owner of the local Columbia fishing fleet, had introduced this new idea at the exhibition to promote fish sales.

In July 1887, the partnership with Pullen was dissolved and Nightingale now became fully responsible for the Royal Aquarium. Ten years later, in April 1897, he became the proprietor instead of the lessee and later that month he was given a dinner by notable persons in the town in recognition of the great part he was then playing in the growth of attractions and the general well-being of the town. He was described as being *an indispensable part of Yarmouth life, both on the civic and pleasure side*.   He held a seat on the Council for the Regent Ward from 1899.

One of the Bass trains arriving at Great Yarmouth

By the turn of the century, Nightingale had become involved in almost every major entertainment business and large hotels in the town. His energy and foresight made him one of the most important and influential figures in the development of Great Yarmouth as a seaside resort in the years around the turn of the twentieth century. As an impresario and director of theatres, he was associated with some of the most famous artists of the day and as an entrepreneur he ran successful businesses as a refreshment contractor and hotel proprietor. His ability to organise large dinners led to him being invited each November to the Mansion House, London, for the Lord Mayor's ball. Nightingale had few equals and his fame was known all over the country.

It was entirely due to the efforts of John Nightingale that the huge Bass outings, described as the *largest outings in the world*, came to Great Yarmouth five times between 1893 and 1909. On each occasion up to 15 trains brought up to 10,000 people on a day's excursion to the seaside. Nightingale arranged a wide ranging programme of events to cover the day and provided the catering facilities for breakfast, lunch and tea.

After a prolonged illness John William Nightingale died at his home, 67 Marine Parade, on 26th June 1911, aged 61 years. He left a widow, a son and a daughter. The funeral took place on 1st July and he was buried in the Gorleston Cemetery. The local paper described him as *a man who has left an indelible mark upon the modern history of Great Yarmouth* and *if ever the term Prince of Business was deserved by any man it was by Mr. J. W. Nightingale, whose achievements have been on great and spacious lines.*

His son, Walter Hogarth Nightingale, who in 1915 was Vice Commodore, Hon. Secretary and Treasurer of the Great Yarmouth Yacht Club, succeeded him as owner of the Royal Aquarium, Theatre Royal and the Queen's Hotel. Walter eventually sold the entertainment venues, but continued to run the Queen's Hotel until his death on 13 August 1936, aged 61 years. The Queen's Hotel remained in the Nightingale family until the 1950s.

The Royal Aquarium

John William Nightingale was associated with the following businesses in the town.

1. The Royal Aquarium had opened in 1876, but in its early years was not a financial success. It closed as an aquarium in 1882 and, after much rebuilding, reopened as a theatre and catering establishment with Nightingale as lessee. The main hall could accommodate 1,000 diners and the minor hall, 400. Some of the original fish tanks were retained in the corridors. It became the Royal Aquarium after the Prince of Wales' many visits.

2. Shadingfield Lodge was built as a summer villa by James Cuddon in 1865 this had become the Nightingale family home in 1873. The Nightingales continued to provide accommodation

for the Prince of Wales, who had first stayed there in 1872 and on subsequent occasions when he was in the town in his role as Honorary Colonel of the 2nd Norfolk Prince of Wales Own Artillery Militia. The Prince, an enthusiastic theatregoer, attended many performances at the Theatre Royal and Aquarium, arranged by John Nightingale.

Shadingfield Lodge

3. The Theatre Royal was built in 1778 for £1,000. The money was raised by eleven £100 subscriptions, for which the backers were rewarded with silver tickets, allowing them free access to the theatre at any time. The theatre closed in 1889 and was bought by Nightingale for £1,200. He bought back the original silver tickets, renovated the building and brought it back to a first-class theatre, re-opening it in 1892. Four shops were added on the Regent Road frontage of the building.

4. The Assembly Rooms were built in 1862 as the Assembly and Reading Rooms. The building was bought in 1879 by the Norfolk Artillery Militia as their officers' mess. Nightingale was appointed the caterer for all the functions and regimental dinners, many of which were attended by the Prince of Wales. When the Prince of Wales Norfolk Artillery was dissolved under the Army reorganisation of 1908, the building was bought by Nightingale. The regimental silver was sold and Nightingale was given the custody of the 102 Coats of Arms of the officers who had served in the Regiment which decorated the Mess Room. The Assembly Rooms then became a Masonic Lodge, of which Nightingale was a member.

5. The Victoria Hotel was built by the Victoria Building Company in 1841, as part of a prestigious development designed to bring upper class people to the town. The hotel was modernised in 1895 by the addition of hot water apparatus and later bought by John Nightingale. In the 1950s it became the Carlton Hotel.

6. The Royal Hotel was opened in 1840, the first seaside hotel in the town. It was partly rebuilt in 1877 and was later bought by Nightingale.

7. The Queen's Hotel was built in 1884 by the brewers Steward & Patteson to replace an older hotel, having the same name, on the corner of Apsley Road and Regent Road. Nightingale bought the hotel in 1897 and, as owner of the Victoria, Royal and Queens, he now became the leading hotelier in the town.

8. The original Britannia Pier was built in 1858 but, after suffering damage by two ships colliding with the wooden structure, was demolished in 1900. The New Britannia Pier Company, a company formed by Nightingale and which he was Managing Director of, rebuilt the pier, opening it in 1901. An elaborate pavilion was built at the end of the new pier, opening in 1902. This pavilion was destroyed by fire in 1909 and Nightingale resigned. It was said that the destruction of the pavilion hastened the death of John Nightingale two years later.

9. The Warwick Revolving Tower was built near the Britannia Pier in 1897. It was sold in May 1902 to a newly created company, the Great Yarmouth Revolving Tower Company for £2,032; the Managing Director of this company was John Nightingale, who was a major shareholder. The tower, one of only five built in this country, was demolished in 1941.

Colin Tooke

Shrublands Farmhouse

Magdalen Way, Gorleston
Unveiled by the Mayor, Councillor Malcolm Bird
Introduced by Julian Macey RMS
Sponsored by Councillors Marlene Fairhead and Babs Wright for
Gorleston-on-Sea Heritage
23rd September 2016

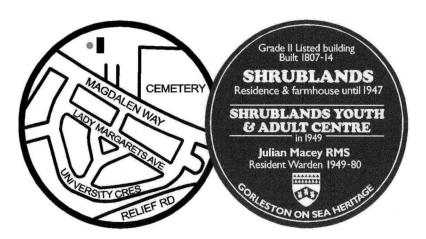

The Shrublands Farmhouse was built by Thomas Thurtell between 1807 and 1814 and remained a private residence until 1947. Amongst its notable tenants were Rear-Admiral Sir Eaton Stannard Travers and William Danby Palmer. At one time it stood in six acres of landscaped grounds.

After the Second World War, in 1947, the Borough Council acquired land that belonged to Magdalen College, Oxford, in order to promote the building of a large housing estate to re-house families that were bombed out, living in temporary accommodation or returning home when they were de-mobilised from the forces. It was inspired forward social thinking to acquire the Shrublands farmstead and land to create open space for recreation and buildings to be developed as a community centre for residents of all ages.

So began the Shrublands Youth and Adult Centre which opened in 1949. In June 1949 the education committee appointed Julian Macey as its warden with the task of developing social and recreational activities. He served at the centre from 1949 until 1980, and is widely-credited with pioneering the centre's success.

For its time it was a bold new experiment, to have activities for all ages at the same centre. Local people and businesses were trusted to undertake a great deal of voluntary work to convert the farm buildings to a theatre, sports hall, changing rooms and utilise every room in the farmhouse, including the cellar, for activities of almost every imaginable sort for everyone from toddlers via youth to elderly. So successful was the centre that 80,000 attendances were recorded in the 1960s.

Today, many of the original community buildings are still in place and extensively used, together with the original farmhouse and the cottage plus some new more modern dedicated buildings.

The farmhouse is listed Grade II.

Les Cockrill

David and Anna Hinderer
Pioneer Missionaries

The Old Vicarage, Black Street, Martham, Norfolk
Unveiled and introduced by the Bishop of Norwich, the Rt. Rev'd. Graham James
Sponsored by Martham Local History Society
18th June 2017

The Anglican missionary Anna Hinderer died in Martham in 1870. Anna Hinderer, nee Martin, was born in Hempnall in Norfolk in 1827. Her mother died when she was five years of age and she was brought up in Lowestoft by relatives. She had an ambition to be a missionary and on 14th October 1852 she married David Hinderer. He was from what is now Germany and was employed as a missionary to Africa by the British Church Missionary Society. In 1852, they both set out to establish a new mission at Ibadan in what is now Nigeria. In 1853, they arrived in Ibadan and, although they had intended to travel further, they decided to set up their mission there.

Anna Hinderer

Ibadan's population was around 100,000 according to David. Anna taught in the school that they had built, looked after orphan children and she ran the mission when David was away preaching or attempting to translate the New Testament into the local language. During the years at the mission, Anna and David endured the most horrendous ordeals of isolation, illness and starvation and tribal warfare. In 1860, war broke out and the hostilities prevented them from being able to travel to the coast for five years. Money and food ran out and Anna Hinderer's health suffered and she returned to England in 1869. She died in Martham in Norfolk in 1870, where her husband was an assistant curate.

Anna Hinderer's gravestone to the east of the church had degraded over the years and in many places was illegible. It has been restored by the Great Yarmouth stonemason, Colin Smith, and was re-dedicated by the Bishop of Norwich on the 18th June 2017. Earlier, the Bishop unveiled a blue plaque to Anna and David Hinderer on the Old Vicarage.

Anna Hinderer has a small stained-glass window devoted to her in the Lady Chapel of Liverpool Cathedral depicting twenty-one Noble Women. Recently a book, *Anna Hinderer, Pioneer Missionary,* written by Ann Meakin has been published.

Ann Meakin and Paul P. Davies

The Bishop of Norwich blessing the Hinderer's grave

The restored grave of Anna and David Hunderer

The Hinderer part of the twenty-one noble women window in Liverpool Cathedral

William 'Billy' George Fleming GC (1865 -1954)
Much decorated Coxswain of the Gorleston Lifeboat

11 Pavilion Road, Gorleston
Introduced by Jim Carter, President of the Great Yarmouth and Gorleston Lifeboat
Unveiled by Paddy Lee, present Coxswain of the Great Yarmouth and Gorleston Lifeboat
23rd October 2017

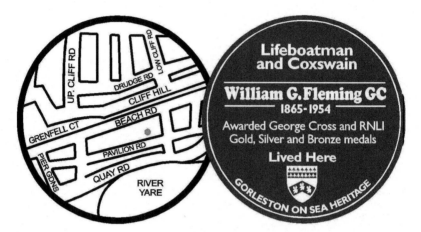

Billy Fleming

Coxswain Billy Fleming is second only to Henry Blogg as the most decorated Norfolk lifeboatman.

Born in Gorleston on 26th July 1865, he married Annie F. Hickman at Great Yarmouth in 1906 and died in Gorleston on 30th September 1954 aged 89 years. Growing up on Lower Cliff Road, Gorleston, he and his father were fishermen working on the East Coast. Billy Fleming first volunteered as a member of the lifeboat crew in the mid-1880s.

Billy and Annie Fleming lived at 11 Boundary Road (now Pavilion Road) most of their married life.

Billy Fleming was appointed as Coxswain of the Gorleston Lifeboat in 1922, when he was about 57 years old and held that position until 1934. Over his 50 years of service in the Royal National Lifeboat Institute (RNLI) lifeboats and in the volunteer boats he assisted in the rescue of 1,188 people.

Awards received by Billy Fleming :

1. RNLI Gold Medal: awarded in 1922 for his part in the rescue, on the 19th to 21st October, of the crew of *SS Hopelyn,* which was aground on Scroby Sands. A mayday was received by the Gorleston oar-powered lifeboat, *Kentwell.* Coxswain Fleming received a tow for the lifeboat from a tug and they progressed through 40 foot waves. All that could be seen was a small part of the *Hopelyn* and there was no sign of life. However, the lifeboat stood off the wreck all night. At daybreak, there was still no sign of survivors, so the *Kentwell* returned to the shore. An hour later a flag was seen flying from the *Hopelyn* and the *Kentwell* made for the wreck again. Near the *Hopelyn,* the *Kentwell* was thrown onto Scroby Sands by a large wave and later severe damage was caused to the lifeboat by being hurled against the hull of the *Hopelyn.* The Lowestoft motor lifeboat *Agnes Cross,* was launched and the two lifeboats met. Fleming, who had now been at sea for 16 hours, transferred on to the *Agnes Cross*. The Lowestoft

lifeboat now approached the *Hopelyn* as darkness closed in. After a time the conditions forced the *Agnes Cross* to return to the shore. The next morning, with a strong gale still blowing, the *Agnes Cross* returned with a mixture of Lowestoft and Gorleston crewmen, including Fleming. At the wreck of the *Hopelyn*, the lifeboat was maneuvered alongside it and the crew scrambled down ropes on to the *Agnes Cross*. The rescue had taken a total of 30 hours, two lifeboats, and one tug, but all 23 crewman, the captain and the ship's cat were all rescued safely

2. RNLI Silver Medal: awarded in 1927 for his part in the rescue of the crew of the Dutch tanker *SS Georgia*, which was stranded on Haisborough Sands on the 21st November. Additionally, he was awarded a silver watch, with a letter of thanks to the crew of the lifeboat, from the Queen of the Netherlands.

3. RNLI Bronze Medal awarded three times: one award was in 1926 for the rescue on the 22nd December in a gale and heavy seas of four seamen from the ketch *Henrietta*.

Billy Fleming

Following the *Hopelyn* rescue, Billy Fleming was awarded the EGM (Empire Gallantry Medal) for which both he and Henry Blogg, the Cromer Lifeboat Coxswain, were gazetted on the 30th June 1924; the EGM was converted to the George Cross in about 1941.

Les Cockrill

The wreck of the Hopelyn. Courtesy of Peter Allard

The Artillery Volunteers' Drill Hall

Artillery Square, Great Yarmouth
Unveiled and introduced by Hugh Wiltshire
(The grandson of an officer who trained at the hall)
Sponsored by Patricia Page (Chair of First Move Furnishaid)
1st December 2017

Artillery Hall

The Artillery Hall was built in 1880 on an open piece of land off Nelson Road Central. Originally the area was known as Somerset Place and was later renamed Artillery Square. The Drill Hall was built of red brick with York stone settings and was 73 feet long by 40 feet wide. Orderly and committee rooms were attached, each 17 feet by 13 feet. The architect was Mr. Arnott of Hall Plain. In 1906, an extension of two stories was added to the west of the building. Several large openings were cut through the west wall to give access to the extension. A new external doorway was provided at the north end. The concrete floor of the extension was designed, with grooves and a channel to clear horse droppings and to allow horses to be accommodated in that part of the building. The first floor of the extension was divided into rooms with access by a metal staircase in the north-west corner of the original building. At the rear of the extension an external metal staircase was provided from the first floor. This was made by local iron founders, Pertwee and Back. This staircase was replaced in 2005. The building was used by the military until the 1950s. Internal partitions and ceilings have been added by subsequent users, but the main fabric of the building remains.

In 1858, the country appeared to be on the verge of war with France and, in May the following year, the Government authorised the formation of Rifle and Artillery Volunteer Corps. These forces were in addition to the Militia, who had been re-formed five years earlier. The Volunteers were liable to be called out in case of actual invasion. Each man was required to attend 28 days drill or exercise in a year. The Artillery Corps were raised to man coastal guns and forts in Great Yarmouth.

On 28 September 1859, a Garrison Artillery unit, known as the 1st Norfolk Artillery was formed in Great Yarmouth. Although a Rifle Volunteer Corps had been formed a few weeks, earlier there was no lack of recruits for the artillery. By 1867, the Rifle Volunteers had raised enough finance to build the York Road Drill Hall. By the end of the year, 65 men had enrolled in the Artillery and it soon became possible to form two Companies or Batteries of Garrison Gunners. Volunteers had to raise the money to buy their uniforms. The dress uniform worn by the Artillery Volunteers was a dark blue tunic with sky blue facings, edged with white cord and was worn with a bearskin busby with a white plume. The Battery's first headquarters were at the Corn Hall in Howard Street, at the rear of the Duke's Head Hotel. Two outlying detachments were formed, in Ormesby and Reedham, each with their own 32-pounder gun.

Doors to the drill hall

The Artillery Volunteers were authorised to fire the guns of the North and South Batteries for firing practices. A week's annual camp was held, often on the South Denes, with other volunteers attending from other parts of the country.

By 1879, the Artillery Corps had raised enough funds (about £600) by selling shares of £1 each to build their drill hall, which was completed in 1880. The hall could be used for other purposes, for example, for exhibitions and concerts. Later that year the Volunteers from Great Yarmouth, Norfolk and Suffolk were united into a single corps: the 1st Norfolk

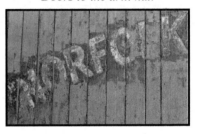

Artillery Volunteers and the Drill Hall was used nightly for drill practice.

In 1889, the artillery were provided with four 16-pounders guns and limbers and were now a mobile horsed unit. The horses were hired as required. At the 1894 annual inspection, 128 men were on parade with their 16-pounders and they fired at targets in the sea 1,400 yards away.

Artillery volunteers with a 16-pounder and limber

Over the years the Artillery Volunteers were reorganised and renamed. Several men enlisted to fight in the Boer War. Following a series of fund raising events an extension to the Drill Hall, giving more floor space with offices above, was completed in 1906. When war broke out in August 1914 the Battery was mobilized and served in France, Egypt, Palestine and Jordan. The Battery continued into the 1930s with exercises and camps and became motorised. Their drill hall was now inadequate and new premises were built in Southtown Road in the late 1930s. During the Second World War, the original hall was used by the Home Guard. After the war the hall was used by National Service men and cadets. In the 1950s, the building was handed over to the borough council and was used by various bodies. Finally, in 1997, First Move Furnishaid occupied the premises.

Colin Tooke

Gorleston High Street Methodist Chapel

The William Adams (J. D. Wetherspoons)
Unveiled by the Mayor, Councillor Kerry Robinson Payne
In the presence of William Stewart Adams, William Adams great great grandson
Sponsored by Gorleston-on-Sea Heritage
23th March 2018

Built in 1807, the High Street Methodist New Connexion Chapel was the first purpose built Methodist chapel in Gorleston. Earlier Methodist places of worship had been converted from other premises. In 1812, it become a Wesleyan Methodist Church following the growth in numbers of the Wesleyans.

By 1843, the old chapel had become too small to meet the needs of the growing congregation and it was demolished to enable the building of a larger and more impressive building. The new Wesleyan High Street Methodist Chapel opened in 1844.

In 1853, for various financial reasons, Spelman and Sons, Auctioneers, were offering for sale the freehold building known as the Wesleyan Chapel. It was purchased by the Wesleyan Reformers, another schism of Methodism, and, in 1854, opened as a Wesleyan Reform Chapel.

In 1873, it became a United Methodist Free Church when the several factions of Methodism united.

About 1881, the building was sometimes referred to as the Temperance Hall or the Templers' Hall, having become the base for the Star of Gorleston Lodge of

Gorleston High Street Methodist Chapel

Good Templers. However, within a few years it was again referred to as the Free Church Chapel, although the Star of Gorleston Lodge of Good Templers still held some activities there.

The United Methodist Church was formed in 1907 and that is what the High Street Chapel continued as until it was bomb damaged in the Second World War. It officially closed in 1948. After standing unused for many years it was sold for £700 and demolished in 1959 to help to fund the building of the Methodist Church on the Magdalen Estate. One fragment remained as the back wall of GT Motors shop and workshop.

While clearing the site prior to building the J. D. Wetherspoon Bar and Restaurant to be called the William Adams, workman unearthed a brick vault with an arched roof which was found to contain two coffins. The two bodies were unidentified as the nameplate, due to corrosion, was illegible. Both remains were sealed in zinc lined, hermetically sealed caskets. The deceased were re-interred in a private plot at Gorleston Old Cemetery.

Les Cockrill
A plaque commemorating William Adams was placed on 199 Bells Road in 2004 and is described in the book Plaques in and around Great Yarmouth and Gorleston.

An unknown couple from the Gorleston Methodists

The brick vault surrounded by orange netting and the gravestone in Gorleston Old Cemetery

Ruth Vincent (1874-1955)
Operatic Prima Donna

56 Market Place, Great Yarmouth
Introduced by Paul P. Davies
Unveiled by the Mayor, Councillor Kerry Robinson in the presence of Ruth Vincent's great
great great niece, Maria Cubitt.
27th April 2018

Ruth Vincent

The precise date of Ruth Vincent's birth is uncertain, but was probably 1874 and she was christened Amy Ruth Bunn the daughter, one of ten children, of the butcher Henry Vincent Bunn and his wife Emma. In 1871, Henry Bunn was a marshman at *Amos Farm*, Acle Road, Runham. It was here that Ruth Vincent was born. A year later Henry Bunn moved to 56 Market Place as a butcher.

Little is known of Amy Ruth's singing career in Great Yarmouth. The Norwich newspapers note that in 1888 she sang a song at a Priory School concert and sung in a concert at St. Andrew's School Room.

From, not a rich large family, how Ruth Vincent came to have singing lessons, presumably privately in Norwich, is unclear. From the census returns the family could not afford to employ any live-in servants.

However, Dr. Horace Hill, a singing teacher of Norwich, was walking along Southtown Road, where the Bunn family were living at the time. He heard a girl singing so sweetly that he knocked at the door and asked to see the singer to whom he made an offer of three years free tuition, which she accepted. She later studied under Herman Klein. Klein introduced her to Columbia records in 1906 and she became one of their regular recording artists. She went to London and took the stage name of Ruth Vincent. Based on the quality of her voice she obtained the position of understudy to the principal soprano in an opera being performed at the Savoy Theatre, then occupied by the D'Oyly Carte Opera Company.

Ruth Vincent's actual debut as a soprano was in the chorus of *The Chieftains* at the Savoy Theatre in December 1894 when she was 20 years old. She went on tour with the company in 1895 returning to the Savoy in 1896 as an understudy. She slowly established herself as the chief lyrical soprano on the English Stage taking major parts in several Gilbert and Sullivan operettas, including: *The Yeomen of the Guard* (at the age of 23 years), *The Gondoliers, The Sorcerer, H.M.S. Pinafore* and many operettas now forgotten. Sullivan saw her in a later Savoy production of *The Lucky Star* and he noted in his diary, *Ruth Vincent looked as if she were furious at being relegated to the chorus.* In November 1899, Sullivan's *The Rose of Persia* was premiered. Dismayed when she was not selected for the leading soprano role, Ruth Vincent rejected the smaller part she was assigned and left the D'Oyly Carte for good, one week before the opening. This was one of the few times anyone had ever walked out at the Savoy. *Miss Vincent threw up her part, silly girl,* Sullivan wrote in his diary. She then went to New York and took the leading soprano role in *The Rose of Persia*, but the show was closed after 25 performances in September 1900.

Ruth Vincent married Lieutenant Colonel John Fraser of the Royal Horse Guards, who was a stockbroker. They lived in Finchley Road in some style. She gave up the stage for two years after her marriage but continuing vocal studies in Paris. She returned to the West End stage in 1903 appearing in many musical comedies. She was *described as the Queen of the London Palladium.* In 1910, She appeared with the Thomas Beecham Opera Company and at Covent Garden in *Hansel and Gretel* (as Hansel), *Così fan Tutte* (as Fiordiligi), *The Tales of Hoffmann* (as Antonia), *Don Giovanni* (as Zerlina), *A Village Romeo and Juliet* (creating the role of Vrenchen, the Juliet role, in Delius's opera) and *Carmen* as Michaela. She went on a concert tour of the provinces in 1911 performing in performances of the Messiah and Elijah.

Ruth Vincent received glowing acclaim by the critics, such as:

London has been crowded for months to see Miss Ruth Vincent. One of the many reasons for the decline of the popularity of comic opera was the want of a prima donna. This no longer exists as Miss Vincent, who held the position in the 1870's and early 1880s, still holds it today.

Seldom indeed has Miss Ruth Vincent's silver voice poured itself out more lavishly than in some exquisitely fresh and dainty love songs.

At a concert given in the Sutton Rectory grounds, Norfolk on a very calm evening, the voice of Miss Ruth Vincent, who sang several songs, was heard distinctly three miles away.

One of Ruth Vincent's sisters, Great Yarmouth born and bred, Margaret Vincent Bunn was the actress and singer, Madge Vincent. She served in the D'Oyly Carte chorus and in musicals on the London stage in minor parts.

Another sister, Agnes Vincent was also a singer on the London stage. Robert Vincent Bunn, a brother of Ruth Vincent, was also a singer.

So, four of the ten children of Henry and Emma Bunn became professional singers, based in London. While they were treading the boards, the others, as far as one can ascertain stayed in Norfolk.

Ruth Vincent did appear occasionally in Great Yarmouth, mainly at Britannia Pier, booked by J. W. Nightingale and, as he stated: *at great expense*, and also at concerts at the Town Hall.

She retired from the stage in 1930 and died in London in 1955 aged 81 years.

Her large suitcase of coffee colour leather that had belonged to the celebrated opera singer Ruth Fraser (known as Ruth Vincent) was sold at auction at Christies in London on 25th January 2000 for £80.

Ruth Vincent's voice can be heard on You Tube singing:
Comin' thro' the rye (1906) https://www.youtube.com/watch?v=0NQ2Nxg93Ko

Paul P. Davies

Hanse Kontor

26 South Quay, Great Yarmouth
Introduced by Paul P. Davies
Unveiled by the Mayor, Councillor Kerry Robinson
27th April 2018

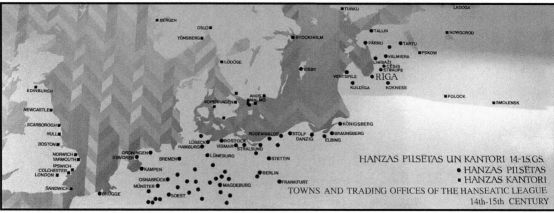

TOWNS AND TRADING OFFICES OF THE HANSEATIC LEAGUE
14th-15th CENTURY

The Hanseatic League, also called Hanse, was an organisation founded by north German towns and German merchant communities abroad to protect their mutual trading interests. The League dominated commercial activity in northern Europe from the 13th to the 15th century. Hanse was a medieval German word for guild. The origins of the League are to be found in groupings of traders and groupings of trading towns in two main areas: in the east, where German merchants won a monopoly of the Baltic trade, and in the west, where Rhineland merchants (especially from Cologne) were active in the Low Countries and in England. The League came into being when those various associations joined together with Lübeck, having a central position. Northern German mastery of trade in the Baltic Sea was achieved quickly and was completed in the late 12th and the early 13th centuries. The Swedish island of Gotland, was soon established as a major centre for trade in the Baltic and for the Russian trade. German merchants helped establish important towns on the east coast of the Baltic: Riga in Latvia, Tallinn in Estonia and Danzig (now Gdańsk) in Poland. Thus, by the early 13th century Germans had a near monopoly of long-distance trade in the Baltic. The dominance achieved by German traders came about as towns, who had a common interest in foreign trade, formed Hanses with each other. These towns were dominated by great merchant families and they passed laws to remove obstacles to trade. In 1241, these towns formed alliances to secure action against robbers and pirates.

In the meantime, merchants from Cologne and other towns in the Rhineland had acquired trading rights in Flanders and in England. In London, by the end of the 10th century, they enjoyed royal protection and with their increasing trade in England during the 12th century their privileges increased and many Cologne merchants lived in London. Privileges were granted by Henry II in 1157 and Richard I in 1194 in return for financial aid.

In the last half of the 13th century, the trade of the Baltic and the North Sea was in the hands of German merchants. Grain, timber and pitch, tar, potash and charcoal, wax and honey, and hemp and flax all were traded from the south and east of the Baltic (modern day Russia and Poland) and shipped to the industrial west (Flanders and England), which in turn sent cloth and other manufactured goods eastwards.

The major aims of the Hanseatic League were:

- Firstly, they wanted their trade to be secure in northern and eastern Europe with action against pirates and land robbers.
- Secondly, they provided lighthouses, marker buoys, trained pilots, and other aids to safe navigation.
- Thirdly, they formed bases abroad and secured favourable terms.
- Fourthly, they established a monopoly in trade.
- Fifthly, it was a political organisation to oppose competitors.

The 14th century was marked by strong resistance from local merchants, who were strong enough to try to oust the foreigners and there was a stagnation of trade. This at times led to warfare, such as against the Danes.

The League had no permanent governing body, no permanent officials, and no permanent navy, no central treasury and no central court. It was governed by irregular meetings that met usually at Lübeck. The membership of the League was essentially a membership of towns. At the League's peak, about the middle of the 14th century, the total number of participating towns certainly surpassed 100, but generally it was less, and it tended to decline in the 15th and 16th centuries. To qualify for membership a town had usually to be German, independent, represented at meetings, and a prompt payer of all dues imposed. There were exceptions with foreign towns participating in its privileges, such as Stockholm and towns in Poland and groups of merchants, resident as far away as Iceland, Ireland, and Spain. The other essential elements in Hanseatic organisation were the Kontor, a foreign trading post. The Kontors owned a large complex of houses, halls, warehouses, and other buildings, where they lived a severely disciplined life and carried on their trade with the natives. In the 15th to 17th centuries, the League declined. The London Kontor was deprived of its privileges by Elizabeth I in 1598 in retaliation for the Holy Roman Empire placing restrictions on English traders. The Hanseatic League also declined through the increasing power of nations such Denmark, England, Prussia, Russia, Sweden and the Dutch Republics. Also, trade became moved away from the North and Baltic seas to the Atlantic and the wider world. Their last diet or meeting was held in 1669.

There is little or no mention of trading with the Hanseatic League in Great Yarmouth's extensive archive. However, we learn from Henry Swinden's book, the *History of Great Yarmouth* that: *the merchants of the Hanse had commerce with Yarmouth for herrings etc. and disputed paying the customs.* There appears to be no date attached to this note. However, it is clear that Great Yarmouth once hosted a Hanseatic Kontor.

Paul P. Davies

Arthur Henry Patterson (1857-1935)
Associate of the Linnean Society, Naturalist, Journalist, Author and School Truant Officer

Time and Tide Museum, Blackfriars Road, Great Yarmouth
Introduced by Michael Pearson, Chairman of the Great Yarmouth Naturalists' Society and the President of the Great Yarmouth Wildfowlers' Association
Unveiled by the Mayor, Councillor Kerry Robinson in the presence of Arthur Patterson's great granddaughter, Brenda Pawsey
27th April 2018

Arthur Patterson was born in 1857 at 8 Garden Row (Row 36). His mother died of tuberculosis when he was three years old. His father later re-married. Arthur was the only child of eight to survive over the age of 21 years. Arthur's father was a shoemaker and a strict Primitive Methodist and Arthur attended its school. Later, Arthur became a Methodist lay-preacher. He spent his spare time with his father on his allotment at Runham, where his interest in the natural world began. He was able to see Breydon Water from the allotment's shed roof and with his friend he began to explore it and also the seashore around the town.

Arthur Patterson

He began to write books on Natural History, his first book being *Seaside Scribblings*. He wrote articles for the *Yarmouth Gazette*. He was well-known for his pen and ink sketches, which he drew very quickly. He owned three houseboats, which were locally known as *Noah's Arks*. Their names were *Moorhen 1, Moorhen 2* and *Moorhen 3*. His last houseboat was situated on the north side of Breydon Water at Duffell's Rond.

Although Arthur did not shoot birds in his later life, he respected the old boys who made a living wildfowling on Breydon Water.

In his early days, Arthur had several jobs. He worked as a storeman at Palmer's Department Store and his boss, J. Hurry Palmer, took Arthur shooting at Martham. His other jobs were:

selling tea, an insurance agent, a sewing machine salesman, a postman, a ticket attendant and a zoo keeper. In 1892, he was appointed the school attendance officer, a post he held for 20 years.

At the age of 39 years, he used the pen name, *John Knowlittle*, when writing for newspapers. He was well-known as a Broadland naturalist and most of his homes were called *Ibis House* or *Ibis Lodge*.

Arthur's main love, apart from his family, was Breydon Water. He later wrote *Wildfowlers and Poachers*, which the young Ted Ellis (later to become a famous naturalist himself) typed out for the printers. Ted Ellis greatly respected Arthur Patterson and Ellis attended all the Great Yarmouth Naturalist's Society Christmas socials with his wife, Phyllis, until his death.

Arthur took very many trips on Breydon and the Norfolk Broads in his Breydon gun punt called *Yarwhelp* (the local name for the bird, the black-tailed godwit).

Row 36 Garden Row
An unusual Row with gardens

He was appointed an Associate of the Linnean Society and he died in 1935 and was buried in Gorleston Cemetery with a pen placed in his hand by his son, John.

Michael Pearson

Arthur Patterson and
Yarwhelp

A. H. PATTERSON,
Naturalist.
Ibis House,
Gt. Yarmouth.

With
"John Knowlittle's"
Compliments

a h Patterson 1919

Medieval Guildhall
Gorleston's oldest house

32/33 Baker Street, Gorleston
Introduced by Les Cockrill
Unveiled by Bernard Williamson, Chairman of the Great Yarmouth Preservation Trust
Sponsored by Gorleston-on-Sea Heritage
18th April 2018

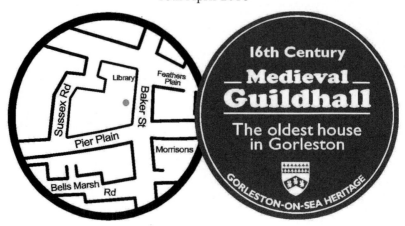

Nos. 32 and 33 Baker Street, Gorleston is a late Medieval building with evidence of alterations dating from the 17th to the 20th centuries, which include the replacement of the queen post roof being replaced in the 18th century. There is a tentative 16th century date for the building and it was probably a Medieval hall. It probably consisted of at least one heated and one unheated room. Later in the 16th century a rear range was added. The building has a full height timber framed rear wall and a timber framed and jettied first floor above a masonry front wall. The chimney stack is off-centre towards the street side of the building, a characteristic usually associated with stack-side stairs. Hundreds of years ago it was at the hub of local democracy as Gorleston's Guildhall, when the High Street passed its front door running from the parish church to the quay, taking in a smattering of manor houses.

The former Medieval Guildhall

By 1992, the property was in terminal decline and it was purchased by the Great Yarmouth Preservation Trust to save it from demolition. They paid £23,000 for the property and the cost of repairs amounted to £173,000. The finance was derived from grants: £20,000 from Living over the Shop, Great Yarmouth Borough Council, £5,750 from English Heritage, £40,000 from

English Heritage Buildings at Risk, £2,000 Historic Buildings Grant, and £95,000 Architectural Heritage Fund. The renovated building became a shop, now a hairdressers, on the ground floor with living accommodation above.

The renovated building was opened by Baroness Hollis of Heigham in 1995.

Les Cockrill

32 and 33 Baker Street prior to restoration

21

The Priory of St. Nicholas, Great Yarmouth
Benedictine Priory founded 1101, dissolved 1539 and a school

Priory Plain, Great Yarmouth
Introduced by Sue Salter
Unveiled by David Parsley, the head boy of the Priory School in 1956
Sponsored by the Priory Community Trust
8th September 2018

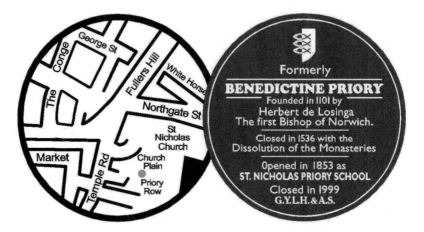

Formerly
BENEDICTINE PRIORY
Founded in 1101 by
Herbert de Losinga
The first Bishop of Norwich.

Closed in 1536 with the
Dissolution of the Monasteries

Opened in 1853 as
ST. NICHOLAS PRIORY SCHOOL
Closed in 1999
G.Y.L.H. & A.S.

In 1101, Bishop Herbert de Losinga (1094-1119) founded the parish church of St. Nicholas and with it a small Benedictine cell under the control of Norwich Cathedral. The monks (three chaplains and a deacon appointed by the prior) served the parish church. The priory establishment was later increased to a prior and eight monks with a number of singing men until the Reformation. The priory was enlarged in 1260.

The great hall of the priory and St. Nicholas Church

The only surviving part of the priory is the great hall of 1260, which was probably used as a refectory. The hall is 60 feet long and 30 feet wide. A minstrels' gallery was erected at the east end of its south side. A stone screen, bearing the arms of East Anglia, Ancient France, England with Castille and Leon, divided the hall from the buttery. The screen is an extremely fine and rare survival. It consists of a five-bay arcade. The four large windows with tracery light the hall and are contemporary with the screen.

At the Dissolution of the Monasteries, the priory remained under the control of the Dean and Chapter at Norwich Cathedral. In 1551, they leased the priory to Robert Sowel for 80 years. The prior's lodgings were demolished at the time of the civil war and the cloisters were used for storing powder and shot. The cloisters were demolished in 1811 and the shields of the arms of France and England were removed from the priory screen and were inserted on the front of the south porch of St. Nicholas' Church.

The great hall of the priory being used as a stable (Cotman)

Many of its other buildings were converted into cottages. The great hall was filled with so much rubbish that access could only be gained through a window. The hall was used as a stable by one of the local doctors. A hay loft ran through its entire length. It is thought that the Old Vicarage stands on site of the priory's gatehouse.

Following the fall of the suspension bridge over the River Bure in 1845, when many children drowned, money was raised to convert the great hall into a school and extensions were built in a Gothic Revival style, The school, maintained by the Church of England, opened in 1853.

Many notable people have stayed at the priory, including Richard II in 1382 and Mary Tudor, the daughter of Henry VII in 1515. In 1578, Elizabeth I cancelled her visit to the priory as the plague had broken out in Norwich. She sent Lord Leicester and Lord Cecil in her place.

The school established in 1853 catered for boys and girls of all ages. In 1958, the senior children located to the Styles School leaving the school as St. Nicholas Priory Church of England voluntary aided primary school. This school amalgamated with the Hospital School

The great hall after its restoration in 1852

and re-located to the Market Place in 1999. The priory complex then became the Priory Community Trust and after financial difficulties it was sold to a private enterprise.

Paul P. Davies

22

The Town Battery

Prom Hotel, Marine Parade, Great Yarmouth
Introduced by Paul P. Davies
Unveiled by the Mayor, Councillor Mary Coleman
29th September 2018

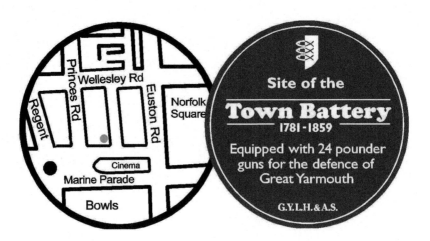

Being on the coast and close to Europe, Great Yarmouth required defences.

The town wall was constructed and was completed at the end of the 14th century. By then it was obsolete, because of the advent of cannons. The wall was not thick enough to mount artillery upon it, so several gun platforms, called mounts, were constructed. The first mount was built in 1569 on St. George's Plain, to the east of the later built St. George's Church.

Great Yarmouth built a new fort at the haven entrance in 1653 during the First Dutch War. The fort had to be repaired at least twice. The inside area, excluding the two bastions, was only 76 feet square. The south bastion of the fort was undermined by the sea and collapsed in 1822 and the remainder was demolished in 1834.

As by now the town wall was inadequate as a defence, three batteries; the North Star, the South Star (so called as they were star shaped) and the Town were built in 1795. An additional battery was later sited in Gorleston. The Gorleston battery was demolished around 1816, and its site is under the junction of Upper Cliff Road and Cliff Hill.

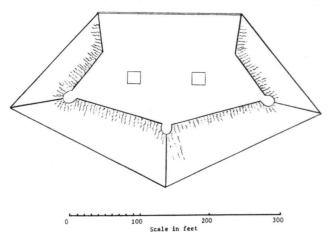

Town Battery. Courtesy of Colin Tooke

The batteries were built during the American Wars of Independence against the French, the Dutch and the American enemies. They were well-built solid earthwork structures surrounded by a wide ditch revetted with wood. There were wooden blockhouses. Being near the beach the works were troubled with windblown sand. After building a brick platform a ditch was dug around it with the sand being built up around the platform with turf covering it to keep it in place.

The North Star Battery, a fortified

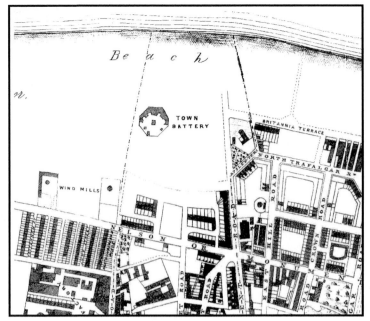

Laing's Map of Great Yarmouth 1855

gun emplacement, was built in 1795. It later fell into disuse, but was reconstructed in 1811, and eventually equipped with 32-pounder guns. The battery was then subject to periods of disuse followed by sporadic renovation and re-fortification until it was demolished in 1922, the resulting rubble being used in the building of Beatty Road. Barnard Road was built across its north edge

The South Star Battery was built in 1795 and was finally demolished in 1924. The site is now occupied by the south end of Harbord Crescent. It was repaired at least twice. In 1859, the battery had seven guns (five 68-pounders and two 24-pounders) with the larger cannons weighing 95 cwt. moving on pivots. It was still in use in 1914.

The Town Battery was built in 1781 in a hexagonal shape and was demolished to make way for the extension of Marine Parade northwards in 1858. In the same year, the materials belonging to the town battery were sold for £84. 12s. 0d. In 1858, the Great Yarmouth Borough Council, after negotiations with the Board of Ordnance, exchanged the site of the Town Battery for a site further east. An extraordinary proposal, as in this year the Britannia Pier was opened, which was in front of the battery. In the event the new battery was not built and the old battery was demolished in 1859, and now lies underneath the houses on Marine Parade, between Paget Road and Euston Road.

Town Battery.
Picture enlarged from a beach scene dated 1857.
Courtesy Norfolk Museums Service

It is unlikely that any of the guns were fired in anger, but they were used for gunnery practice, being fired at targets in Yarmouth Roads by the volunteers, the militia and their ilk. They were also used to give salutes.

Paul P. Davies.

23

Captain Thomas Kisbee RN (1794-1877)
Inventor of the life and breeches buoy

26 Victoria Road (former Claremont Terrace), Great Yarmouth
Introduced by Paul P. Davies
Unveiled by the Mayor, Councillor Mary Coleman
29th September 2018

Thomas Kisbee was born in Farset, Huntingdonshire in 1794. He joined the Royal Navy in 1808 and obtained a commission in 1826. He was appointed as a coastguard at Great Yarmouth in 1827, where he stayed for 15 years. Later he became the Chief Coastguard Officer and lived at Beach Watch House, Great Yarmouth and was involved in many rescues. At this time, he developed the idea for a life buoy to supplement the rocket apparatus earlier devised by Manby and Dennett.

In 1841, as a Lieutenant he was transferred to *HMS Driver*, a steam warship. She was 1,058 tons and 280 horse power, carrying four large guns, two 68-pounders and two 84-pounders with a crew of 175 men, including marines. She set sail for China to partake in the First Opium War between 1842-43 and then was ordered to New Zealand. In 1846, *HMS Driver* arrived there via Hong Kong, Swann River, Hobart and Sydney. She was the first steamer to visit the colony and excited much interest. .On returning to Portsmouth, via Rio de Janeiro in 1847, Kisbee had participated in the first steam paddle ship to circumnavigate the world and had sailed 75,600 miles. During the voyage 32 men had died.

In 1848, Thomas Kisbee was promoted to Commander and he was later retired with the rank of Captain. He then moved to 26 Claremont Terrace, Victoria Road, Great Yarmouth.

Kisbee breeches buoy

It was reported in 1841, that Thomas Kisbee had constructed and brought into practice an apparatus for saving lives from stranded vessels. The apparatus was light and simple and could be carried to a wreck by two or three people and was useful when the first communication had been effected by means of Manby's or Dennett's Rockets. The apparatus consisted of a net made of small line capable of bringing a woman and child, or a man with his bag onto the shore. A float or circular buoy, its diameter 32 to 34 inches, circumference 19 inches and made of common rush was covered with unbleached calico, dressed with three coats of oil or thin paint. It weighed six to seven pounds and was quite sufficient in keeping a man's head and shoulders above water. A pair of petticoat trousers made of stout canvas was attached in front and back of a hoop attached to the Kisbee's Ring, the waistband being 14 inches, supported a man. So in effect it is an early Breeches' Buoy. This was been tried twice in the sea off Great Yarmouth in 1841. Kisbee had also developed a sort of telegraph with words "Look for a line", "Haul in if ready", "Shout" etc.

Kisbee's floats and buoys had severe trials at Great Yarmouth through very heavy surf in 1840 and 1841 and they were highly approved off by numerous scientific and nautical men who witnessed the experiments.

In 1842, by order of the Lords of the Admiralty, Kisbee's life-saving apparatus was tested. The esplanade in front of Kimberley Terrace at South Beach, Great Yarmouth was thronged with spectators. Kisbee's float was used when a sailor from *HMS Defence* revenue cruiser was hauled to and fro between the jetty and the shore.

In October 1847, Royal Naval ships were fitted out with Kisbee's life buoys for trail and the officers were requested to report on the quality of the buoy at the end of the year.

In 1862, the Admiralty directed that two of Kisbee's new life buoys are to be supplied to each ship in commission.

Yarmouth July 1877 and May 1897

In July 1855, Thomas Kisbee was awarded the silver medal of the Royal National Lifeboat Institution for his gallant conduct in assisting the rescue of 199 people shipwrecked on the Norfolk coast. He had received many honorary rewards in acknowledgement of his brave services. The citation read: Thomas Kisbee has invented a useful float or life buoy, which has been useful in saving lives.

In 1840, the Royal International Shipwreck Institution at Paris presented an honorary medal to Kisbee for the zeal, skill and courage manifested by him in saving lives from shipwreck on the coasts of Norfolk and Suffolk on several occasions in by means of his apparatus. He was their Honorary Vice President .

Thomas Kisbee died on 27th May 1877 aged 83 years and was buried in the Old Cemetery. After Kisbee died in 1877, his house was auctioned when his address was stated as 26 Claremont Terrace, Victoria Road. Twenty years later, 26 Claremont Terrace, Victoria Road was auctioned again, when a description of its location was given: on the corner of Victoria and Duncan Roads. The house is now 26 Victoria Road.

Paul P. Davies.

24

Sir Robert Harry Inglis Palgrave FRS FSS (1827-1919)
Economist, Banker, Author and Statistician

54 Marine Parade, Great Yarmouth
Introduced by Paul P. Davies
Unveiled by the Mayor, Councillor Mary Coleman
29th September 2018

Robert Harry Inglis Palgrave

Sir Robert Harry Inglis Palgrave (known as Inglis), was educated at Charterhouse School, but did not go to a university. He was the son of Sir Francis Palgrave and his wife Elizabeth Turner, who was the daughter of the banker, Dawson Turner. He was named after his godfather, Sir Robert Harry Inglis, the Member of Parliament for Oxford University. Inglis Palgrave's father was an eminent historian and his work, *The Rise and Progress of the English Commonwealth* became a classic.

Inglis's father, Sir Francis Palgrave (1788-1861) was born Francis Ephraim Cohen in London, the son of Meyer Cohen, a Jewish stockbroker, who was financially ruined in 1810 in a stock market crash and Francis, his eldest son, became responsible for supporting his parents. Francis was a child progeny and became a lawyer and in 1838 he was appointed deputy keeper of Her Majesty's Records and is considered to be the founder of the Public Record Office. In 1819, he made the acquaintance of the banker Dawson Turner and his daughter Elizabeth at the house of the Quaker banker, Hudson Gurney and he offered to correct the proofs of Turner's book, *Architectural Antiquities of Normandy*. In 1821, Francis Cohen was admitted to the Fellowship of the Royal Society, one of his sponsors being Dawson Turner. Francis Cohen converted to Anglican Christianity before his marriage to Elizabeth Turner in 1823. He changed his name from Cohen to the maiden name of his future mother in law. She was the granddaughter of William Palgrave of Coltishall. It is not clear if either the religious conversion or his name change were conditions of his marriage. However, his father-in-law, Dawson Turner, paid for the expenses of the name change, and settled £3,000 on the couple. Sir Francis Palgrave is buried at Irstead Church in Norfolk.

In 1843, Francis' son, Inglis Palgrave at the age of 16 years, joined the bank of Deacon,

Williams and Company in London, where he was groomed to replace his grandfather Dawson Turner at the bank in Great Yarmouth. In 1845, he joined Turner and Gurney Bank in Great Yarmouth. Gurney's Bank amalgamated with Barclay and Company in 1896.

From the electoral registers, we find Inglis Palgrave living in Great Yarmouth at Britannia Terrace (Marine Parade) at least from 1869 to 1883. From the town directory and the census returns, we learn that the house number was four in the 1860s. On the census returns by 1871 and 1881 he had moved to 11 Britannia Terrace.

Britannia Terrace has been absorbed into Marine Parade. On Laing's map of Great Yarmouth dated 1855 we see that eight houses of Britannia Terrace have been built and these were at the north end, so it is probable that the terrace was numbered from the north.

In 1859, Inglis Palgrave married Sarah Maria Brightwen, the daughter of George Brightwen of Saffron Walden.

Inglis Palgrave began publishing in the late 1860s. His 1871 essay won a prize from the Statistical Society of London. His 1873 treatise, focusing particularly on bank statistics, set him out as one of the leading authorities on banking matters and spokesman of the country banks. In 1875, Inglis Palgrave gave testimony to the House of Commons on banks of issue (that is banks empowered by government to issue currency). In 1877, Inglis Palgrave became the financial editor of *The Economist* and became editor-in-chief in the same year, a position he held until 1883. He edited the collected historical works of his father, Sir Francis Palgrave. He also edited *The Banking Almanac* until his death, and for a time he was the editor of *The Bankers' Magazine*. He was elected a Fellow of the Royal Society in June 1882. He was knighted in 1909 and the year after he received the Freedom of Great Yarmouth.

In 1885, Inglis Palgrave was appointed one of Her Majesty's Commission on the Depression of Trade and Industry, to which he contributed an appendix to the report. He wrote many publications including *Notes on Banking in Great Britain and Ireland, Sweden, Denmark and Hamburg* and for this work was honoured by the King of Sweden with the Order of Vasa.

But, perhaps Inglis Palgrave's principal claim to fame is editing the comprehensive three volume *Dictionary of Political Economy*. He gathered a distinguished group of international contributors, and the three volumes originally appeared between 1894 and 1899. This was a landmark in both publishing and economics: a liberal and scholarly overview of the whole sphere of economic thought in its day. Henry Higgs's revised edition, *Palgrave's Dictionary of Political Economy* (1923-6), retained the spirit of the original publication while embracing new concepts in the development of economics as a discipline. A four volume *The New Palgrave: A Dictionary of Economics* was published in 1987 to international acclaim. Obviously, its scope had expanded and evolved almost beyond what Palgrave himself would have recognised. Well into the 21st century it remained a standard work for economists. In 2008, Palgrave Macmillan published *The New Palgrave Dictionary of Economics*, 2nd edition.

In Great Yarmouth, Inglis Palgrave's activities in committee work were numerous. Great Yarmouth owes to Inglis Palgrave the preservation of the Greyfriars Cloisters, which he purchased and handed over to trustees for the public.

Inglis Palgrave died in Bournemouth in 1919, where he was spending the winter. His body was brought back to Fritton and he was buried alongside his wife in Fritton churchyard. He left £47,450 (approximately one million pounds today). The Times wrote that: *he was, indeed, the grand old man of British banking and banking literature.*

Inglis Palgrave was the last of four famous sons of Sir Francis Palgrave. The Palgraves were an extraordinary family; four brothers who in widely separate fields each earned recognition.

Paul P. Davies

Miles Corbet's House
English Politician and Regicide, 1595-1662

26

68 Market Place, Great Yarmouth
Introduced by Andrew Fakes
Unveiled by the owner of the house, Dr. Ken Seymour
4th May 2019

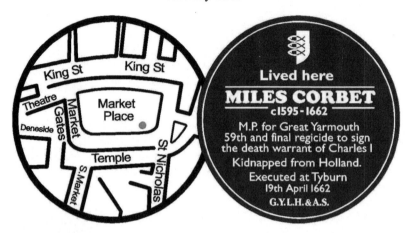

Lived here
MILES CORBET
c1595-1662
M.P. for Great Yarmouth
59th and final regicide to sign
the death warrant of Charles I
Kidnapped from Holland.
Executed at Tyburn
19th April 1662
G.Y.L.H.&A.S.

Miles Corbet

Miles Corbet was the second son of Sir John Corbet, a Norfolk baronet. Miles was elected the Recorder of Great Yarmouth in 1625 on the condition that he lived in the borough. He was elected the Town Clerk from 1631 and the Member of Parliament for Great Yarmouth from 1640 to 1653. He lived in a house on the east side of the Market Place. In the Parliament of 1628, he was appointed to the High Court of Justice.

During the English Civil War, Great Yarmouth supported the Parliamentary cause. Corbet was a lawyer to and a personal friend of Oliver Cromwell, who was a frequent guest of John Carter (commander of the militia in the town) at 4 South Quay. Discussions are believed to have taken place concerning the execution of Charles I at 4 South Quay in 1648. Corbet was one of the judges at the trial of King Charles I in 1649 and was the last signatory on the King's death warrant. King Charles I was executed in Whitehall on 30th January, 1649.

At the Restoration of the Monarchy in 1660, Great Yarmouth Corporation was purged of Parliamentarians. Corbet escaped to Amsterdam and, with his companions, Barkestead and Okey, fellow regicides, moved on to Rotterdam in an attempt to rescue their families. However, they were betrayed by Sir George Downing, the ambassador, who had formerly supported the Parliamentarians. They were captured at Delft, brought to England, tried and condemned to death. They were hung, drawn and quartered at Tyburn on 19th April 1662. Pepys recorded in his diary that he saw them in Aldgate being taken to their execution and that they looked very cheerful. He heard that they had died defending what they had done to the former King, which Pepys found to be strange. In his dying speech he said: *When I was first called to serve in parliament I had an estate; I spent it in the service of the parliament. I never bought any king's or bishop's lands; I thought I had enough, at least I was content with it; that I might serve God and my country was that I aimed at.*

Andrew Fakes

Great Yarmouth Lions Club Holiday Home for the Blind

1 Avondale Road, Gorleston
Introduced and unveiled by Rodney C. Holland-Merten
President of the Great Yarmouth Lions Club
Sponsored by Gorleston-on-Sea Heritage
25th August 2018

The home was purchased by a board of trustees on behalf of the Great Yarmouth Lions Club. These same trustees were responsible for the funding of the home and the appointment of a full time warden. A warden was appointed and the home, the first for the blind in the country, opened its doors for holidays on 2nd June 1959.

Lion Clubs from all over the country would apply for holidays and a draw would take place to see which clubs were lucky to have been picked and how many places they required. A further draw would then be taken to allocate the dates. It was the responsibility of each individual club to provide transport to and from the home.

Members of the Lions painting the holiday home for the blind in 1959

The home was reliant on the Great Yarmouth Lions Club for its running costs. This home was the sole beneficiary of a *Win a Car Competition*, run by the Great Yarmouth Lions Club. This competition took place every year on the sea front in Great Yarmouth with a new car being the sole prize. To take part you had to guess how many people would attend the National Motor Show held in London each autumn. The winner was then brought back to Great Yarmouth and a presentation of the car took place at the club's annual Charter Celebration, followed the next day by a visit to the Blind Home, where they received their new car.

Unfortunately, this type of competition went out of favour with the public and in June 1992 the home was sold, although the holidays still took place for a few years after this.

Rodney C. Holland-Merten

Margery Kempe (c1373 to after 1438)
Christian Mystic

St Nicholas' Churchyard, Northgate Street Railings, Great Yarmouth
Introduced by Paul P. Davies
Unveiled by the Rector, Rev'd. Canon Simon Ward
4th May 2019

Margery Kempe

Margery Kempe was an English Christian mystic, known for her book written during the 1420s which she dictated to scribes, *The Revelation of Divine Love,* known today as the *Book of Margery Kempe.* This work is considered by some to be the first autobiography written in the English language. Her book chronicles her domestic tribulations, her visions, her religious experiences as well as her temptations to lechery, her travels, her trial for heresy, her extensive pilgrimages to holy sites in Europe and the Holy Land, as well as her mystical conversations with God. Kempe's book was lost for centuries, being known only from extracts. However, in 1934, a manuscript was found in the private library of the Butler-Bowdon family. It fell out of a cupboard when the family were looking for a ping-pong ball. The book has since been reprinted and translated in numerous editions.

Margery Kempe's father was a merchant in Bishop's (King's) Lynn, a mayor of King's Lynn and their Member of Parliament. At around 20 years of age, Margery married John Kempe, who became a King's Lynn official in 1394. She loved fine clothes and good quality jewellery and was a failed business woman.

Margery and John had at least 14 children. Later, she decided to be celibate. Her husband said that it was his right according to 14th century marital law that her body was his, to do with as he pleased. Eventually, after much cajoling, weeping and wailing, Marjory Kempe got her wish, but her husband only agreed to a celibate marriage on three conditions: that they sleep in the same bed, that Marjory pay his debts and that Marjory made him a fish supper on Fridays. From this point Marjory gave herself over to a life of complete religious devotion.

Kempe believed that she was summoned to a greater intimacy with Christ as a result of multiple visions and experiences she had had as an adult. After the birth of her first child, Kempe went through a period of crisis for nearly eight months, perhaps due to postnatal depression or even mania as part of a bi-polar disorder. During her illness, Margery claims that she saw numerous devils and demons attacking her and commanding her to forsake her faith, her family, and her friends.

Kempe said that she had visitations and conversations with Jesus, Mary, God, and other religious figures and that she had visions of being an active participant during the birth and crucifixion of Christ.

She prayed, went to confession two or three times a day, prayed early and often each day in church. She wore a hair shirt and willingly suffered abuse from her community concerning her extreme forms of devotion. Kempe was also known throughout her community for her constant weeping as she begged Christ for mercy and forgiveness. Her loud wailing, sobbing, and writhing frightened and annoyed both the clergy and the laypeople.

Sometime around 1413, Kempe visited the female anchoress, Julian of Norwich, at her cell in Norwich. According to her own account, Kempe said that Julian approved of Kempe's revelations and gave Kempe reassurance that her strong religious belief was genuine and also confirmed that Kempe's tears were a physical evidence of the Holy Spirit in her soul.

Margery Kempe went on many pilgrimages and is known to have purchased indulgences for her friends, her enemies, the souls trapped in Purgatory and herself. In 1413, she left King's Lynn and travelled to Norwich and prayed at Norwich Cathedral and then travelled to Great Yarmouth and prayed at an image of Our Lady Mary in St. Nicholas' Church and then boarded a ship. She landed near Rotterdam and then travelled via Bologna, spent 13 weeks in Venice and then travelled to Jerusalem. She was in Jerusalem for three weeks and went to Bethlehem, Mount Zion, the burial places of Jesus and his mother, Mary. Finally, she went to the River Jordan and Bethany, where Martha, Mary and Lazarus had lived. She returned via Assisi, Rome and Middleburg to England, where she fell to her knees and kissed the ground giving thanks for her safe return.

Kempe also went on pilgrimage to Santiago de Compostela in 1417, travelling via Bristol and also visited holy sites in England and in Danzig, now Gdańsk, Aachen etc. Kempe is honoured in the Church of England on 9th November, but she was never made a Roman Catholic saint.

Paul P. Davies

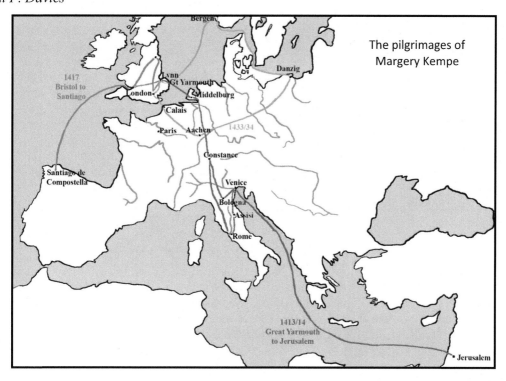

The pilgrimages of Margery Kempe

28 Campbell Archibald Mellon RBA ROI (1876 -1955)
Artist

1 Upper Cliff Road, Gorleston
Introduced and unveiled by Margaret Carver (artist)
Sponsored by Gorleston-on-Sea Heritage
25th June 2019

Mellon was born in Berkshire in 1876. His birth was registered as Archie Campbell Mellon, but the forename, Archibald, seems to have been dropped or moved to his middle name during his adult life.

He worked as a travelling salesman after moving to Nottingham in 1903, where he also undertook some artistic training from Carl Brenner, a nephew of the landscape painter Benjamin Williams Leader. In 1918, after service in the First World War, Mellon moved and settled in Gorleston, initially at 2 Upper Cliff Road, moving to 1 Upper Cliff Road at some time during the 1930s. He met and became acquainted with Sir John Arnesby Brown R.A. (1866-1955). For the next three years, Mellon became Sir John's student and also his friend. Mellon focused on painting seascapes and some of his finest works are of Gorleston beach. He captured the ever changing coastal atmosphere and mood with brilliant tonal qualities, clever use of texture and colour, tending to favour heavy threatening skies. Campbell Mellon became a regular exhibitor at the Royal Academy from 1924 showing a total of 50 paintings. He was elected to the Royal Institute of Oil Painters in 1938 and to the Royal Society of British Artists in 1939. He was also a founder member and the first Chairman of the Great Yarmouth and District Society of Artists.

Late Afternoon, June 1927 by Mellon
Great Yarmouth Museums

Although Mellon's worked out of doors, his paintings were believed to be largely composed in the studio, as he re-arranged and eliminated detail he did not see fitting and added design to suit his ideas. He was more interested in composing an image. Mellon's work can be found in private collections worldwide and can be seen in public galleries in Bristol, Leeds, Sheffield, Norwich and Great Yarmouth. He died in Gorleston in August 1955.

Rowland Fisher RSMA ROI (1885-1969)
Artist

2 Upper Cliff Road, Gorleston
Introduced and unveiled by Margaret Carver (artist)
Sponsored by Gorleston-on-Sea Heritage
25th June 2019

Rowland Fisher was born in Gorleston and lived in Upper Cliff Road for his whole adult life. He was the son of a master mariner, who died when Rowland was a young boy.

Rowland Fisher originally wanted to go to sea, but was instead apprenticed to a timber yard (Jewson and Sons of Great Yarmouth), where he worked for 52 years with 40 years as the mill manager, whilst painting in his spare time. His lifelong love of ships, shown in many of his seascapes, meant that he became an expert ship model maker. He sat for many hours in his house overlooking the harbour observing the waves and the skies.

Fisher is best known for his marine works in oil and watercolour, although he also painted Norfolk landscapes, as well as continental scenes.

He helped to found the Great Yarmouth and District Society of Artists, of which he later became the president. Following painting holidays, he was elected a member of the St. Ives Society of Artists.

He won the Watts prize in 1949 for the best picture portraying men working at sea. He was later made a member of Royal Institute of Oil Painters. He has influenced many of the later East Anglian landscape artists.

There is a representative selection of his work in the Norfolk Museums' collection. He exhibited at the Royal Academy in 1949 as well as in Europe.

Les Cockrill

Sergeant George William Loades
Killed in the First World War

Loades' Court, Newport Road, Hemsby, Norfolk
Unveiled by the Mayor, Councillor Shirley Weymouth
Sponsored by Hemsby Parish Council
2012

George William Loades was born in a house on the site of, what is now, the newly built George Loades Court, off Newport Road in Hemsby, in 1893. He died fighting in France. He is listed on the 1911 census as working as a game keeper, but after that he joined his local regiment, the Norfolk Regiment in Great Yarmouth, and was posted to the 7th Battalion. With his battalion he landed in France on 30th May 1915, taking part in the final phase of the Battle of Loos.

Loades'Court

This battle was the largest British offensive mounted in 1915 on the Western Front during the First World War and marked the first use of poisonous gas by British forces. On 13th October 1915, the 7th Norfolks led the 35th Brigade into a renewed attack on German positions known as the *Action of the Hohenzollern Redoubt.* They did succeed in capturing the gun trench and the south western face of the Hulluch Quarries, but were not able to advance further. It was on this day that Sergeant Loades was killed. The division lost 117 officers and 3,237 men were killed or wounded.

British casualties at the Battle of Loos were around twice as high as German casualties Loade's body was never recovered and his name is listed among the 20,000 names on the Loos memorial as well as on the war memorial in the church grounds of St, Mary the Virgin on The Street, Hemsby.

Great Yarmouth Technical High School
The first purpose built technical high school in England

Oriel Avenue, Gorleston
Unveiled by the Mayor, Michael Jeal
Sponsored by Gorleston-on-Sea Heritage
2nd July 2019

The 1944 Education Act, known widely as the Butler Act, enabled and encouraged local education authorities to organise secondary education on a tripartite system of grammar, technical high and secondary modern schools. This was significant in giving equality of recognition to technical education and the established strand of more classical grammar school education: a very significant step for Britain's post-war regeneration.

Great Yarmouth County Borough's Education Department was at the forefront of this development, indeed many Education Authorities never did establish technical high schools. A senior technical high was established in the former Edward Worlledge Senior School in September 1945 and the age of admission was lowered from 13 years to 11 years in 1946 to align it with the 11 plus examination.

Duke of Edinburgh opens the technical college

In 1947, the Technical High School became the first co-educational school in the Borough and a female member of staff was appointed as the Senior Mistress.

Planning for a new purpose built Technical High School commenced in 1950; but a national shortage of steel delayed progress during 1952 and 1953.

On 2nd December 1954, The Duke of Edinburgh officially opened the school; the first purpose built technical high school in England. The new school admitted boys and girls and promoted a very vocational skills orientated syllabus such as carpentry, metal working, building skills and business and commercial studies.

The Technical High School was renamed in 1997 and became Oriel Grammar School.

Les Cockrill

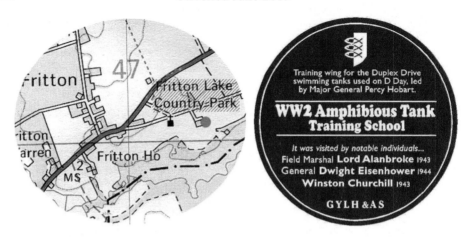

Training wing for the Duplex Drive swimming tanks used on D Day, led by Major General Percy Hobart.

WW2 Amphibious Tank Training School

It was visited by notable individuals...
Field Marshal **Lord Alanbroke** 1943
General **Dwight Eisenhower** 1944
Winston Churchill 1943

GYLH &AS

*Percy Hobart
Imperial War Museum
ref H20967*

In April 1943, Fritton Lake was requisitioned by the 79th Armoured Division as part of the top secret plans associated with the D-Day landings.

Tanks were modified to make them amphibious, to enable them to swim to the Normandy Coast and provide close fire support to the infantry on the first assault wave. Buoyancy was achieved by attaching a collapsible screen, inflatable rubber columns and a tubular framework of steel, which enclosed the upper portion of the tank. Propellers fitted to the rear of the tank provided propulsion when waterborne and also gave the tank its code name: Duplex Drive or D. D. for short.

Their development can be attributed to Hungarian designer, Nicholas Straussler. However, the training and further trials was achieved under the leadership of Major General Percy Hobart KBE., CB., DSO., MC., who was the Commander of the 79th Armoured Division.

Hobart required an inland lake to conduct the elementary training with the Duplex Drive tank, and chose Fritton due to its wooded shores, open water of 180 acres and its proximity to his other top secret facilities at Orford and Sudbourne in Suffolk. Fritton became known as *A Wing* and was referred to as the *Fritton Bridging Camp*. Its cover story involved the transport of vehicles and equipment by means of ferries and Bailey bridges. Even those local to the lake had to sign the Official Secrets Act, preventing them from disclosing any details of what they saw, and inhibiting access to their properties by everyone, except close family and doctors.

Between 6th April and 10 June 1943, engineers undertook the construction of tank parks, mock up landing craft ramps and a hutted camp for personnel. Fifty Valentine Duplex Drive tanks were stationed at Fritton along with workshops and stores. In addition, a special facility was constructed to enable crews to practice escaping from a submerged tank. One hundred and twenty full-time soldiers were stationed here, to instruct the crews, to maintain the tanks and equipment, and to patrol the site.

Over the ensuing months a total of ten regiments attended the *Fresh Water School*. Their intensive training lasted 14 days, and enabled the crews to perfect launching drills, navigating and landing procedures. In addition, the crews had to learn to waterproof the tank, repair the screens and maintain the drive system. There were five British crews, including the 4th/7th Dragoons, East Riding Yeomanry and 13th/18th Hussars; two Canadian Tank Brigades (6th Armoured Brigade (1st Garry Horse) and the 10th Armoured Regiment (1st Hussars) and three United States tank units/battalions (70th, 741st, 743rd). The crews were billeted in hotels and bed and breakfasts in Great Yarmouth whilst at Fritton, before being sent to a second establishment, *B Wing: Salt Water Wing* at Gosport, Hampshire.

Duplex Drive tank with screens down
Bovington Tank Museum (Ref 6377 C5)

It was during the training of the 743rd United States Tank Battalion that Supreme Allied Commander, Dwight D. Eisenhower, along with Field Marshall Alanbrooke met Hobart to inspect the 79th Armoured Division's training facilities on the East Coast.

Eisenhower arrived on the overnight train from London and arrived at 0845 hours at Saxmundham Station in Suffolk on 27th January 1943.

Their first port of call was Hurst Hall at Saxmundham, which was the headquarters of the 79th Armoured Division, where the party were briefed about the secret and experimental nature of Hobart's division. Visits and demonstrations of the various specialised equipment was conducted, including a tank that destroys mines (Sherman Crab/Flail Tank), Armoured Ramp Carrier (for overcoming sea walls and concrete obstructions) and the Crocodile (a flame throwing tank that was able to shower gun implements with burning liquids with terrifying consequences). The modified tanks were nicknamed, Hobart's Funnies.

Lastly, Hobart, Alanbrooke and Eisenhower visited Fritton. Not only did they witness the various stages of training, including an amphibious tank escape, but also Eisenhower rode on a Duplex Drive Valentine into the lake via one of the landing craft mock ups. It is recorded that he stood on the commander's platform and operated the rudder, steering the tank during manoeuvres.

Duplex Drive tank with screens raised
Imperial War Museum ref H20967

The effectiveness of the Duplex Drives was proven on D-Day when 176 Duplex Drives were launched into the English Channel in the early hours of 6th June 1944 and 121 landed successfully on the five assault beaches. Never before had tanks participated so early in an assault, and, to use Hobart's words: *these tanks proved to be the key to unlocking the gateway to Europe*.

Stuart Burgess

33

Anna Sewell (1820-1878)
Novelist

Church Plain, Great Yarmouth
Sponsored by Mr. Leonard the owner of Anna Sewell House
Unveiled by the Mayor, Councillor Adrian Thompson
28th November 2021

Anna Sewell

Anna Sewell was born in Great Yarmouth the daughter of Isaac and Mary (nee Wright) Sewell.

Mary Sewell was born at Sutton in Suffolk, the daughter of a Quaker farmer and was educated first in a dame school, then by a governess and finally at a Quaker boarding school in Tottenham, London. During her childhood, her father sold his farm and moved his family to Southtown Road in Great Yarmouth where he worked at shipbuilding. However, her father returned to farming in Buxton, near Aylsham in Norfolk, after losing his money in a packet-steamship project, which had failed. The family were active in the Great Yarmouth Quaker community, which included the parents of Isaac Sewell as Elders. Mary Wright had married Isaac, in 1819, at Lammas Quaker Meeting House near Aylsham.

Mary and Isaac Sewell set up home in Church Plain in Great Yarmouth, where Anna was born in 1820, but they left the town for London soon after her birth, as Isaac had financial difficulties. There, the shop he set up was also unsuccessful and Mary hated living in the city. After the birth of their son, Philip, in 1822, her health was such that she was advised to move out of the city, into the country. They went first to Hackney, then to Dalston, where they remained for ten years, with Isaac earning a modest living as a commercial traveller for a lace company. Because of a lack of money for schooling, the children were largely educated at home by their mother. Mary Sewell wrote her first book to buy educational works to help her in this task; she received three pounds for it. The family had moved to Stoke Newington where the children started school. This gave Mary time to be involved in anti-slavery campaigns and visiting the poor. However, Anna's fall on a wet pavement at the age of 14 years damaged both her ankles and led to permanent lameness. This meant that Mary became Anna's nurse. She sought possible cures for her daughter, but to no avail. For greater mobility, Anna Sewell frequently used horse-drawn carriages, which contributed to her love of horses and concern for the humane treatment of animals.

In 1836, Isaac became a bank manager and they moved to Brighton. Over the next 20 years, they moved around Sussex and then to Gloucester, where Mary was baptised into the Church of England, but wherever they lived, she was always involved in helping the poor (although they were not a wealthy family), in mothers' meetings, working men's institutes, prison visiting and the temperance movement.

Mary Sewell's strong belief in moral education for children led to her career as a successful author. She admired the great poets, but made no such claim for herself, although her works were mainly written in verse. In 1858, the publishers of *Jane Eyre* issued her first major book, *Homely Ballads for the Working Man's Fireside*, which was very popular. So, she followed it with *The Children of Summerbrook*, which Jarrold of Norwich published in 1859. Jarrold published all her subsequent books, written in verse or as ballads, but her prose work, *Patience Hart's First Experience in Service,* was the greatest success. This book was about a country bred girl going to London, which reflected the situation of many young girls at the time.

Anna Sewell's brother, Philip, had worked as an engineer in Spain for a number of years, but returned to England to live in Norwich with his wife and family. In 1866, his wife died, leaving him to care for his seven children, so Mary Sewell decided she, Isaac and Anna should move back to Norfolk in order to help him. In 1867, they moved to the *White House* in Catton, Norwich. Mary Sewell wrote no further books, but cared for her immediate family, visited her siblings at Buxton and continued her charitable interests.

By now, Anna Sewell was confined to bed or a sofa, but had started to write *Black Beauty*, either dictating to her mother or writing outline notes, which her mother transcribed. The novel was published by Jarrold, who paid £40 for it, in 1877. Anna Sewell was in extreme pain and completely bedridden for several months, and she died on 25th April 1878 from hepatitis or tuberculosis, only five months after the publication of *Black Beauty*. She was buried on 30th April 1878 at the Quaker burial-ground in Lamas.

Although *Black Beauty* is now considered a children's classic (one of the top ten best-selling novels for children ever written), Anna Sewell originally wrote it for those who worked with horses. She said a special aim was to induce kindness, sympathy, and an understanding of the treatment of horses. In many respects the book can be read as a guide to horse husbandry, stable management and humane training practices for colts. It is considered to have had an effect on reducing cruelty to horses; for example, the use of bearing reins, which are particularly painful for a horse, was one of the

Anna Sewell's birthplace House exterior altered in the 1920s

practices highlighted in the novel, and in the years after the book's release the reins became less popular and fell out of favour.

In 1984, the graveyard at Lamas was bulldozed and the gravestones of Anna Sewell, her parents and maternal grandparents were subsequently placed in a flint-and-brick wall outside the old Lammas Quaker meeting house. There is an Anna Sewell memorial fountain and horse trough outside the public library in Ansonia, Connecticut in the United States of America (1892) and a memorial fountain to Anna Sewell is located at the junction of Constitution Hill and St. Clement's Hill in Norwich (1917).

Ann Dunning

A plaque commemorating Mary Sewell was placed on 56 Southtown Road in 2013 and is described in the book More Plaques in and around Great Yarmouth and Gorleston.

34

Dr. John Aikin MD (1747-1822)
Physician, Unitarian and Author

28 King Street, Great Yarmouth
Erected March 2020

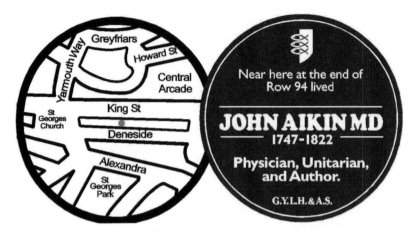

Dr. John Aikin lived in Row 94 (from King Street to Deneside), Great Yarmouth, on the northwest corner in a stately house. He was born in 1747 in Kibworth, Leicestershire. He was educated at the Presbyterian Warrington Academy, where his father, Rev'd. John Aikin was a teacher. It was intended that he should enter the ministry, but the weakness of his voice and the liveliness of his temper caused a change in the direction of his career and he opted for the medical profession.

At 15 years of age, he was apprenticed to Mr. Garthshore, a surgeon and apothecary at Uppingham, Rutland. His three years spent there, he found irksome and uninstructive. He later wrote, *what can you possibly do worse with a youth than send him from the comfort of a lettered and civilised home to a master, probably of sordid habits, in a place where he can find none but gross and vulgar company, if he seeks for any, and where drinking and low vice will be the only pastimes offered him. The restraints of morality and religion held me from rushing into degradation and ruin.* Next, he studied medicine at Edinburgh.

In 1766, he became a pupil, for three years, of Mr. Charles White, a skilful surgeon and obstetrician in Manchester, and found himself treated as a gentleman by his family. In 1770, Akin attempted to settle in Chester as a physician, but found that there was little space for a newcomer in medicine. He moved back to Warrington and worked as a physician and a part-time tutor at the academy teaching anatomy, physics and

John Aikin

chemistry. In 1784, Akin took a physician's degree (Doctor of Medicine) at Leiden, Holland. He came to Great Yarmouth in 1784 and was given a friendly reception. He found the comparatively superior education of the clergy made them agreeable company and he became friends with them. Akin found that the other physician in Great Yarmouth was already well-established and that the town was not big enough to support two physicians (as opposed to surgeons) and friends suggested that he set up practice in London, which he did in the following year. Scarcely had he started practice there when the physician in Great Yarmouth retired, and Aikin accepted an invitation, signed by the leading inhabitants of Great Yarmouth, to return to the town. It was then that he purchased the house, which he described as a very good and pleasant one. Aikin wrote: *the invitation was drawn up and signed by almost everybody of all parties in the town, promising their upmost support. Such a testimony of respect and attachment could not but move me. I was compelled therefore, to accept and return.*

When the French Revolution came Aikin supported it, along with many of the most enlightened community, as it would establish liberty, equality and fraternity. In 1780s, Great Yarmouth society was hostile to dissenters. In 1790, Akin was anxious for the repeal of the Corporation and Tests Acts, which were under discussion in Parliament. The Corporation Act of 1661 excluded from public office those who refused to take Holy Communion in the Church of England. The Test Act of 1673 was designed to exclude non-conformists from civil and military office. Office holders had to receive the Anglican Communion and to affirm the monarch's supremacy as the head of the Church and repudiate the Roman Catholic doctrine of transubstantiation. These acts were not repealed until 1829. On this subject, Aikin, whose political and religious views conformed to those of the dissenters, published two pamphlets against the Acts, and therefore, lost the support of most of his more orthodox friends and patients. The pamphlets were published anonymously, but Aikin was soon identified as their author. His professional prospects in Great Yarmouth were virtually ruined. In a letter to a friend he wrote: *I had no idea of becoming a hero of the cause, but at my age it would be trifling not to have character and cowardly not to avow and stick to it.* His position, ruined by his pen, in Great Yarmouth became more and more intolerable and in 1792 he moved back to London and was in easy reach of Hackney, then the stronghold of dissenters, where he found a more agreeable field for his literary and medical work.

In 1771, Aikin recognised the spread of infection and the connection with poor ventilation. It was observed that inflammation and gangrene were more prevalent in crowded London hospitals than in private practices and country infirmaries. Aikin advocated cleanliness, fresh air, space between beds and the disposal of contaminated clothing and dressings. In 1784, Aikin wrote, *Yarmouth is recommended by a striking air of cheerfulness and neatness. The manners of the lower classes are remarkably decent and civilised. The cry of the night watchman, NNE is the wind, became very familiar.* In one of his letters Aikin stated: *the grand sight of 500 ships at anchor in Yarmouth Roads waiting for a southern breeze had lost its effect upon him from its familiarity.*

Aikin's career as a physician was cut short by a stroke. He retired to a country residence and eventually to Stoke Newington in London. There he spent the last 24 years of his life in study and died in 1822, aged 74 years. His wish *to not live longer than I can use my pen* was not fulfilled, as he slipped into senility in his final years. A contemporary of the time described him as a man of talent and of the highest personal worth, one of the salt of the earth.

His varied attainments earned him many friends, including Darwin, Southey, Walter Scott, Charles Lamb, Coleridge, Wordsworth, Sidney Smith and Josiah Wedgwood. Akin had a long personal association with John Howard. Aikin felt he owed his inspiration to Joseph Priestly, one of the discoverers of oxygen, who taught at the Warrington Academy. Aikin assisted William Wilberforce in the abolition of the slave trade.

Akin wrote the following books: *England Delineated, Materia Medica, Political Pamphlets, An Address to the Dissenters of England on their Late Defeat, Poems, Essays on Song Writing, A Translation of the Germania and the Agricola of Tacitus, Journal of a Tour through Surrey, Observations on the External use of Preparations of Lead, Woodland Companion, An Account of British Forest Trees, A Journal of a Tour through Holland, Annals of the Reign of George III, The Life of John Howard, prison reformer, Evenings at Home, General Biography* (10 volumes), *The Life of John Selden and Letters from a Father to his Son* etc.

Paul P. Davies

35

Lucy Akin (1781-1864)
Author, Historical Writer, Biographer and Unitarian
28 King Street, Great Yarmouth
Erected March 2020

Lucy Aikin was the daughter of a physician, Unitarian and author, John Aikin, who resided in Great Yarmouth in the 1780s. She was born at Warrington and moved to Great Yarmouth at the age of three years. She moved with her parents to Stoke Newington when she was eleven years of age, where she lived until the death of her father in 1822, when she moved to Hampstead.

Lucy Aikin, in her early life, was a diligent student of French, Italian and Latin and at the age of 17 years she began to contribute articles to magazines and reviews. When she was 29 years old, she published her first significant work, *The Epistles on Women.* She gained her reputation by writing historical biography. She was, like other members of her family, a Unitarian. At Great Yarmouth, because of her Unitarianism, she suffered persecution as child, along with her father. While living in Hampstead she began corresponding over a period of 16 years with a fiery Boston Unitarian preacher, named William Ellery Channing, who was known for giving passionate sermons.

Lucy Aikin

Like her aunt, Anna Laetitia Barbauld (a writer of poetry, essays and children's books), Lucy Aikin was interested in early education, and as such published several works to assist young readers by using words of one syllable. She also published under the pseudonyms Mary Godolphin, I. F. M. and J. F. W.

Lucy Aikin died at the age of 83 years in January 1864. She was buried in the churchyard at Hampstead.

Lucy Aikin write a memoire of her father in which she relates about life in Great Yarmouth and her journey from Warrington. *I had just completed my third year when my father decided on a removal from Warrington to Yarmouth. My grandmother, her maid, my little brother, and myself were packed into a post chaise; my father accompanied us on horseback. It was Christmas week, the snow deep on the ground; the whole distance was 240 miles across country, and we were six days in accomplishing it. The last night we arrived at my aunt's, Mrs. Barbauld's house at Palgrave, where my grandmother remained behind with manifest symptoms of decay. She died a few days later of cold and fatigue.* Later Lucy Aikin wrote; *the arrival of a new physician in Yarmouth, already a writer of some distinction, of polished unaffected manners and endowed with powers and tact that rendered his conversations attractive and acceptable to all, was an event of no small importance in the town. His speedy popularity was reflected upon all members of his family. I was soon in danger of being totally spoiled by flattery. My excellent mother taught me what flattery was and strongly warned me against being led away by it. My first view of the ocean from Yarmouth Jetty filled my little bosom with sentiments too big for utterances and the sea was my never failing source of wonder and delight. The flat sandy land extending to the beach was our daily walk, but so much keener was my delight, when we accompanied my father in his professional drives through the shady lanes of rural villages on the Suffolk side of the town. My father was an admirable observer of nature; not a plant, not a bird, not a wild animal escaped him, and he knew them all and taught his children to know them too.*

Lucy Aikin, described the migration from Great Yarmouth to London *as a blessed change from Yarmouth.* Lucy also wrote at the time: *I have sat for the whole evening at children's parties in Yarmouth while others were dancing. Nobody would dance with me, as I was a Presbyterian* (Unitarian). *I have been pushed, hunted and even struck, as I stood silent and helpless to the cry of Presbyterianism.*

Selected works by Lucy Akin:

1801: Poetry for Children: Consisting of Short Pieces to be Committed to Memory

1804: The Travels of Rolando by Louis Francois Jauffret (translated from the French)

1810: Epistles on Women, Exemplifying their Character and Condition in Various Ages and Nations, with Miscellaneous Poems

1811: Juvenile Correspondence or Letters, Designed as Examples of the Epistolary Style, for Children of Both Sexes

1812: Jean Gaspard Hess's The Life of Ulrich Zwingli (translated from the French)

1814: Lorimer, a Tale (her only novel)

1818: Memoirs of the Court of Queen Elizabeth, published in several editions

1822: Memoirs of the Court of James I

1823: Memoir of John Aikin, MD

1825: The Works of Anna Laetita Barbauld

1827: The Life of Anne Boleyn

1828: An English Lesson Book, for the Junior Classes

1833: Memoirs of the Court of Charles I

1843: The Life of Joseph Addison

1858: The Acts of Life: of Providing Food, of Providing Clothing, of Providing Shelter

1858: Holiday Stories for Young Readers

Works attributed to her as Mary Godolphin:

1867: Robinson Crusoe: In Words of One Syllable

1868: Sandford and Merton: In Words of One Syllable

1868: An Evening at Home: In Words of One Syllable

1869: Aesop's Fables: In Words of One Syllable

1869: The Pilgrim's Progress: In Words of One Syllable

1869: The Swiss Family Robinson: In Words of One Syllable

1870: The One Syllable Sunday Book, etc.

Paul P. Davies

36

The Isolation (Escourt) Hospital

Escourt Road, Great Yarmouth
Erected February 2021

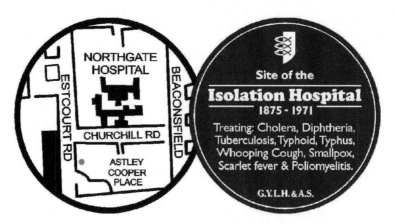

Site of the
Isolation Hospital
1875 - 1971
Treating: Cholera, Diphtheria,
Tuberculosis, Typhoid, Typhus,
Whooping Cough, Smallpox,
Scarlet fever & Poliomyelitis.

G.Y.L.H.&A.S.

In 1875, the Great Yarmouth Health Board requested Dr. Hubert Airey, from the National Board of Health, to visit the town to inquire into the causes for the high rate of infectious disease. As well as detailing the poor sanitary state of the town, Airey recommended that an isolation hospital for infectious diseases was required and this hospital should have an ambulance for the conveyance of sick people, a cart for the removal of infected bedding and clothes, and a suitable apparatus available for disinfection. As a result of the Airey inquiry the Corporation resolved, at the end of 1875, to erect an infectious diseases hospital. The cost was £2,000 and an extra £200 was spent on a high wall 200 feet on each side and seven feet high to enclose it. Later, this hospital was re-named Escourt Hospital after the Chairman of the Poor Law Board. A convalescent ward, a mortuary, a disinfecting house, an ambulance shed, a ward and a laundry with the necessary offices were constructed. There were to be a female and a male ward separated by domestic offices with a storeroom, two bedrooms and a kitchen in the central area. The bedrooms were to be occupied by the resident nurses, a man and his wife. The two wards were to be airy and well-ventilated by six windows and 12 wall ventilators (six near the floor and six near the ceiling) and a large ventilator in the roof. Fresh air and ventilation were thought to be important in the treatment and prevention of disease. Each ward was to be heated by two central stoves with iron pipe chimneys. They were to be lit by gas and furnished

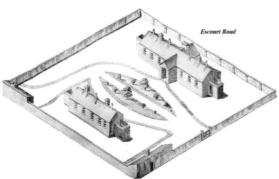

Original plan of Escourt Hospital

with six beds each. The floor of each ward was about four feet above the ground, which was dry sand and the under-floor space was ventilated by six ventilators. They also had open yards at the end for water closets, sinks and water taps. A full-size bath on wheels and furnished with a tap would be used in each ward.

The wooden convalescent ward was to be half the size of the main ward, divided into two to separate males and females, with a room partitioned off for a nurse. It was furnished with six beds. The disinfection house contained a Ransom apparatus powered by gas. The hospital-keeper disinfected, free of charge, any article of clothing or bedding for the public that was contaminated with fever poison.

The ambulance shed contained a cab, which was used to convey patients to the hospital and a large covered barrow for the transit of articles for disinfection. The mortuary was well-lit with gas, well-ventilated, roomy, paved with brick and had a slate table. As well as receiving the dead from the hospital it also received those who had died in the town from infectious disease.

The hospital catered for the following infectious diseases: cholera, scarlet fever, tuberculosis, measles, poliomyelitis, typhoid, smallpox, typhus, diphtheria and whooping cough. It would be many years before these infections were treatable. Cholera and smallpox were treated at various times at other places in the town, viz; the Hospital on the South Denes (c1871-1875), the North Denes Smallpox and Cholera Hospital (1868-?1893) and the Gorleston Smallpox Hospital (c1893-1953).

Due to the sporadic nature of infectious disease, the use of the hospital was variable. For example, in 1892 there were 539 cases of infectious diseases, including 40 cases of smallpox in the town. Ninety-seven cases were admitted to the Isolation Hospital including 28 paupers, whose maintenance was paid for by the Guardians of the Poor. There were 61 admissions whose financial circumstances precluded any payment and eight patients who had their fees paid by their friends or relatives. This, of course, was prior to the start of the National Health Service. During 1898, there were 719 notifications of infectious disease (of which 281 were treated at the hospital). These included 663 cases of scarlet fever, typhoid and diphtheria.

Original ward, Escourt Hospital

The hospital was not free to use by patients and, for example, in 1900 a charge of one guinea a week was made for maintenance in the hospital for those visitors taken ill whilst they were in Great Yarmouth. A similar charge was made to the inhabitants of the town whose houses had a rateable value of over £12 a year. This sum was abated or remitted if the patient or their friends could not meet the cost. The sum of £65 was received from these charges in that year.

In 1894, the isolation hospital buildings were supplemented by a two-ward 80-bedded complex (blocks A and B). The windows on each side of the entrance were at a different height. One of the wards was a children's ward and the lower windows enabled the children to see out.

By 1900, several much needed improvements were made to the hospital. A boiler house was erected for the provision of steam radiators to all the wards. A bacteriological laboratory was built in the hospital grounds and a porter's lodge erected to control the entrance to the hospital and to stop the public wandering about the grounds and thus being exposed to danger. A brougham ambulance was purchased to convey infectious patients to the hospital.

Early in 1904, the Yarmouth Independent reported that the town was in a healthy condition, the death rate was low. These gratifying facts were due to the work of the sanitary officials. They urged the inhabitants of the town, especially those living in hovels, to be clean and pure. In this way there would be less disease, happier families and less pauperism. The misery, now prevalent amongst the poorer families, would be less.

In 1907, an extension for administration and improved nurses' accommodation were built and the isolation hospital consisted of five separate ward blocks and an administrative building. The ward blocks contained 52 beds. A request was made for a loan of £1,050 to extend the administrative building to accommodate the different types of infectious disease. The extension enabled typhoid fever, scarlet fever and diphtheria cases to be separated. The staff consisted of a matron, ten nurses, three ward maids, one housemaid, one dormitory maid, a cook, and a scullery maid. There were only 14 bedrooms for the staff and some rooms had to be used as double bedrooms. This meant that staff, who might be looking after different infectious diseases, had to sleep in the same room. There was only one bathroom, which contained a water closet and three basins for all the domestic staff.

The average stay in the hospital was: scarlet fever, 39 days: diphtheria, 31 days and diarrhoea cases, 41 days.

During the Second World War on 5th August 1940, the hospital was closed and the patients were moved to the East Dereham County Isolation Hospital. In May 1941, ten high-explosive bombs were dropped in the north end of the town and one of the four wards at the hospital was severely damaged.

In 1948, the hospital was taken over by the National Health Service and in that year 257 patients were admitted. These included 93 cases of scarlet fever, one diarrhoea case, five diphtheria cases and 158 unspecified cases. There was a poliomyelitis epidemic and a considerable number of the victims were admitted and it was necessary to have three iron lungs in constant use. In 1950, the Ministry of Health stated that in the event of another local poliomyelitis epidemic, the Isolation Hospital in Great Yarmouth would be restricted to cases of poliomyelitis from the whole of East Anglia and other infectious diseases in the borough were to be treated at East Dereham and King's Lynn Hospitals.

Site of Escourt Hospital and two surviving ward blocks

With the advent of vaccination and immunisation the need for an isolation hospital lessened, but the hospital continued to discharge its prime function for treating infectious disease when required.

From around 1958, the hospital was also used for post-operative care of surgical patients from the General Hospital. For example, in 1961, one hundred and sixty-two convalescent patients were transferred from the General Hospital to the Isolation Hospital. In 1964 the physiotherapy department was moved from the General Hospital to the hospital. Six beds were made available for patients requiring electro-convulsive treatment in 1966, who until now had to be sent to Norwich for the therapy.

In 1971, Mrs. Irene Stoner retired as the last matron. Over the next 30 years the use of the hospital decreased and it slowly deteriorated. In 1970, it was used for the family support team and the health service administration (Primary Care Trust). In 1990, the headquarters of the Great Yarmouth and Waveney Health Authority moved into the former nurses' home. In 1943, an increase in the incidence of venereal disease in the borough led to the opening of a special clinic at the hospital in 1944.

Part of the site now contains housing and the remainder is for sale for development (2022) and many of the hospital buildings have been demolished.

To commemorate the site of this important hospital in the history of the town, the Society has erected a blue plaque on its boundary wall. This compliments the plaques already erected on the site of the borough's General Hospital and the Royal Naval Hospital.

Paul P. Davies

37 Bus Depot, Caister Road
Art Deco Façade

Unveiled by Steve Hewitt of the East Norfolk Transport Users
Introduced and sponsored by Julie Grint
14th August 2019

The Depot was built for trams by Boulton and Paul of Norwich and was opened in 1898.

On 11th and 12th May 1941, a raid on the town resulted in high-explosive bombs dropping to the north of the depot and its roof collapsed and its windows broken. Several buses were damaged. Over two years later, at 08.45 hours on the 12th May 1943 there was a large raid on

Bus Depot

Great Yarmouth, when 20 Focke-Wulf 190 German fighters flew in over the coast. At the depot more windows were broken and two buses were damaged. There was much damage elsewhere in the town. In particular, the Auxiliary Territorial Service Hostel was bombed, and 26 women were killed there. Boulton and Paul quoted £271 for removing the remains of the roof and the depot remained open to the elements for the rest of the war. Four Great Yarmouth buses on loan to Coventry were recalled.

The main work of reconstruction of the depot was completed by 1947. It had been delayed by the Ministry of Transport, who admitted that the work needed to be done, but that materials and labour could not be diverted from the National Building Programme. A compromise was reached with the Ministry by reducing the restoration with exterior work being omitted. F. R. Hipperson and Son Ltd. were contracted to carry out the work at a cost of £19,622 with the War Damage Commission contributing £6,433. It was not until June 1948, that the Ministry of Transport authorised the construction of the final phase, which was the building of the façade. A contract was signed with F. R. Hipperson and Son Ltd. for the sum of £3,376. 4s. 4d. and they constructed a rectangular brick and concrete façade across the complete depot frontage, which disguised the metal framed shed. The façade incorporated sculptured representations of transport vehicles and four cream coloured Deco buttresses. Even though the trams were discontinued in 1933, the tram lines were not removed. Recently the forecourt to the depot was re-surfaced and the tram rails were found to be still in situ.

Julie Grint

ROW 110

Prisoners of War Jail
(1803-14)

n this Row over 4,000 Frenchmen,
Dutchmen and Danes were
ncarcerated during the Napoleonic
War when Great Yarmouth was
a major Royal Navy base.

G.Y.L.H.&A.S.

Row 110 in 1902

During the Napoleonic Wars, Great Yarmouth was a major Royal Naval base. Therefore, a prison was required to house the prisoners of war landed here. In 1793, two fish houses with associated yards with a frontage on to Row 135 were acquired. For some time, it was referred to as Old Prison Row. Large prisons were needed, and one was established in 1797 at Norman Cross near Peterborough and the Great Yarmouth facility became a holding establishment before transfer there. Prisoners were also transferred to hulks at Chatham. With the signing of the Treaty of Amiens by Britain, France, Spain, and the Batavian Republic (the Netherlands) in 1802 the row prison was closed. During the Great Yarmouth Row 135 prison's existence, 3,340 prisoners were held in it of whom 2,700 were transferred to Norman Cross. After the building of Norman Cross Prison, the world's first purpose-built prisoner-of-war camp with a capacity of nearly 7,000, Great Yarmouth became, like Deal and Falmouth, a mere receiving port, but an exceedingly busy one, the prisoners being landed here direct from capture. In a series of articles in the *Norwich Mercury* in the latter part of 1905, Rev'd. G. N. Godwin wrote: *Columns of prisoners, often 1,000 strong, were marched from Great Yarmouth to Norwich and were lodged there in the Castle. They frequently expressed their gratitude for the kindness shown to them by the Mayor and the citizens. One smart captured privateer captain coolly walked out of the Castle in the company of some visitors, and, needless to say, did not return. From Norwich they were marched to King's Lynn, halting at Costessey, Swanton Morley, East Dereham, where some were lodged in the detached church tower, and thence to Lynn. Here they were lodged in a large building, afterwards used as a warehouse, now pulled down. At Lynn they were given water and were conveyed in barges and lighters through the Forty Foot, the Hundred Foot, the Paupers' Cut, and the River Nene to Peterborough, whence they marched to Norman Cross. In 1797, twenty-eight prisoners escaped from the prison at Great Yarmouth by undermining the wall. All but five of them were retaken. In the same year four prisoners broke out of the prison, made their way to Lowestoft, where they stole a boat from the beach and got on board a small vessel, the crew of which they put under the hatches, cut the cable and put out to sea. Seven hours later the crew managed to regain the deck, a rough and tumble fight ensued, one of the Frenchmen was knocked overboard, and the others were ultimately lodged in Yarmouth jail.* [2]

Britain ended the uneasy truce created by the Treaty of Amiens when it again declared war on France in May 1803. Having disposed of the prison in Row 135, another site was required to take 200 prisoners. In Row 110, later known as Prison Row or New Prison Row, two buildings close to each other, previously a malt house, were purchased at a cost of £400 in 1803. The prison staff consisted of four turnkeys, five clerks and ten labourers. Charles Palmer wrote: *all the apertures were bricked up except for a door with an iron grating. Bones were thrown through the grating for the prisoners to carve to pass the time. A sentry was posted at each end of the row and after dusk a password was required to pass down it. Prisoners frequently escaped leading to lamps being placed in the row as a precautionary measure. Alterations were also made to prevent escape through the roof.*

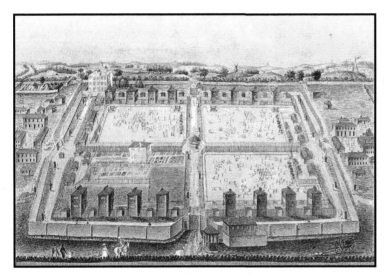

Norman Cross Prison

The first prisoners, five Frenchmen, arrived on 12th December 1803. A day later, 54 prisoners from the privateers *Le Vigilant* and *Lyonois* captured by the gun boat *Vixen* and the revenue cutter *Badger* were imprisoned. Prisoners continued to arrive. For instance, after the fall of Flushing on 16th August 1809, one hundred and eighty prisoners arrived on *HMS Agincourt*. Eleven days later, *HMS Monmouth* arrived with 200 prisoners. A further 200 were brought to Great Yarmouth by *HMS Agincourt* in early September.

Many prisoners of war, especially the Dutch seamen, were exchanged with the British prisoners of war housed on the continent. Some joined the Royal Navy.

The prison along with the Norman Cross Prison closed in 1814. Over 4,000 prisoners had been confined in the Row 110 Great Yarmouth prison. Half were Frenchmen with the remainder being either Dutchmen or Danes in roughly equal proportions.

During the Napoleonic period, more than 100,000 French prisoners of war were held in Britain, and French policy was to force Britain to bear the entire cost of the prisoners in the hope that this would weaken the economy.

Paul P. Davies

39

Peter Henry Emerson (1856-1936)
Photographer, Artist, Naturalist, Physician and Writer

Great Yarmouth Priory, Great Yarmouth
Erected June 2021

Peter Henry Emerson, photographer, artist, naturalist, physician, and writer, died in 1936 all but forgotten by the art world he ignited in the 1880s. It took until 1975 and the publication of Nancy Newhall's book, *P. H. Emerson: The Fight for Photography as a Fine Art*, for the world to realise that he was one of the great pioneers of modern photography and how, through his determination and weight of belief, he had changed the perception of photography for all time.

Peter Henry Emerson

Emerson entered photography in a blaze, casting aside the prevailing artistic attitudes. Convinced, that the photographic discipline had been constrained by an overdependence on topographical accuracy on the one hand and on manipulated pastiches of paintings on the other, he set about challenging the photographic establishment. He championed his technique of differential focusing, where only one part of the image was in sharp focus and all else fell away into being marginally less focused. He worked out an aesthetic based on photography's unique powers. He wrote the first manual on straight photography as an art in its own right, which was aptly described as, *a bombshell dropped at a tea party*. He passionately believed in pure photography and its power to convey 'truth to nature'. He was the first to utilise photography and text to explore the relationship with subject. He was tireless in his pursuit, being a whirlwind, enigmatic, opinionated, and brusque.

He railed against the leading exponents of art photography, saving his fiercest invectives for the likes of Henry Peach Robinson, with their combination prints, classical studies and sentimental pictorialism, that fed into the Victorian ideal of countryfolk and their ways. Robinson felt that it was beneath him to photograph labourers or peasants going about their lives and went to elaborate ends to recreate his saccharine fantasies in his studio.

Emerson meanwhile was explaining to a packed room at the Priory Hall in Great Yarmouth, that art was enslaved except when the artist went to Nature for his subject matter. And he did

Great Yarmouth Harbour
Peter Henry Emerson, Wild Life on a Tidal Water 1890.
Royal Academy of Arts

just that, spending months with his great friend, the painter Thomas Frederick Goodall, moored out on Breydon Water, in view of the *sea-stained* town, in a cranky old houseboat, the *Electra*, and a beery giant of a fisherman called Joey. He records in prosaic detail the characters he meets, or who drop in to visit him. Reading the text of Emerson's *Wild Life on a Tidal Water*, we come to know the fisherman, Harnsee, the hunter Pintail, the smelt fishermen Crab and Cyclops and we join the crowds in the pubs discussing medicinal cures and ghosts.

Emerson was rigorous in his determination and his words and images speak not only for his supremacy as an artist but for those he photographed, and their way of life. Never before had text and image been paired together with equal attention given to both and in the ten years between 1885 and 1895 he produced eight

astonishing portfolios of photographs, blending the scientific with the artistic, and in doing so launched photography itself on to a trajectory from which it never looked back.

He exited the world of photography in as dramatic a way as his entry and, in his enigmatic style, he left the stage with a blistering treatise on the *Death of Naturalistic Photography*. After his last and arguably his best portfolio, *Marsh Leaves*, which he published in 1895, he lay down his cameras and never took another photograph.

Emerson was born on La Palma Estate, a sugar plantation in

Breydon Smelters
Peter Henry Emerson, Wild Life on a Tidal Water 1890
Royal Academy of Arts

Cuba to an American father and a British mother. He spent his early years in Cuba on his father's estate. During the American Civil War he spent some time at Delaware, but moved to England in 1869, after the death of his father. In 1879 he attended Clare College, Cambridge where he graduated with a degree in medicine in 1885.

Mark Cator

40

Great Yarmouth alleged Witches

St. Nicholas' Churchyard, Great Yarmouth
Introduced by Roger Silver
Unveiled by the Mayor, Councillor Adrian Thompson
28th November 2021

September 2020 marked the 375th anniversary of the 1645 witch trials held in Great Yarmouth, which were overseen by the infamous Matthew Hopkins, the self-proclaimed *Witch Finder General*.

Although Witch Mania did not seem to affect the town as it did in other parts of the country, nevertheless 24 allegations of witchcraft were officially recorded over four centuries. Thankfully only seven resulted in convictions which led to execution.

Those accused of witchcraft were quite simply not the besom riding hags accompanied by a black cat riding pillion, as tradition would portray today, but those who simply did not fit in with the society of the day. Throughout history, people down on their luck were forced to turn to begging from neighbours to survive. Those whose political or religious beliefs clashed with others and people falling out of favour with their peers, were found to be at the wrong end of allegations of witchcraft.

In March 1582, Elizabeth Butcher and Celia Atkins were brought before the council at the Great Yarmouth town sessions accused of witchcraft. They were found guilty and the sentence was passed that both women were to be displayed in the town's pillory every market day until they confessed their involvement, then they would be freed. It appears Celia confessed, but Elizabeth was sentenced to imprisonment only to be released upon her confession.

Matthew Hopkins

The following year Elizabeth was again brought before the town sessions, but again denied any attachment to the allegations. Once again, she was placed in the custody of the town's gaoler and at the discretion of the town bailiffs was placed in the pillory until she confessed.

In April 1584, Elizabeth Butcher was brought before the court with another woman, Joan Lingwood. This time the court found both women guilty and they were to be taken to a site of execution at the north of the town. Parish records show that they were buried in St. Nicholas' churchyard on the 18th April 1584.

The 10th September 1645 saw the largest witch trials to take place in the town. Allegations of witchcraft had increased since the beginning of the year. In August, it was decided by Great Yarmouth council officials to send for Matthew Hopkins to come and assist in the proceedings. Matthew Hopkins had been at the Bury St. Edmund's Assizes, where he had discovered 18

alleged witches. Hopkins arrived in Great Yarmouth in early September. After investigation, two men and nine women were accused of allegedly being involved in witchcraft and were brought before the court. The accused were Marcus Pryme, John Sparkes, Elizabeth Fassett, Barbara Wilkinson, Alice Clisswell, Maria Vervey, Bridget Howard, Maria Blackbourne, Elizabeth Dudgeon, Elizabeth Bradwell and Joanna Lacey. The trials pronounced six of the accused women as guilty and they were sentenced to death by hanging. A few days after the trial Joanna Lacey was reprieved. The other five were taken to a site of execution at the north of the town. Parish records once again show the five women, Alice Clisswell, Elizabeth Bradwell, Elizabeth Dudgeon, Bridget Howard and Margaret Blackbourne as being buried in St. Nicholas' churchyard on 29th September 1645.

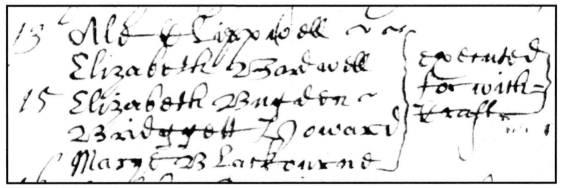

The burial records of St. Nicholas' Church: September 1645 showing the alleged witches' burial

For many, the reason why the alleged witches of 1584 and 1645 were recorded as being buried in the churchyard has been a mystery. Long tradition states that those condemned as criminals, including witches, would normally be buried in unconsecrated ground or at crossroads, where the spirit would be confused and not be able to return and cause mischief in a godly society.

In fact, Christian tradition records that the north side of a churchyard was only used for burial of *outcasts and suicides*. This statement included the unbaptised, excommunicated, strangers and vagabonds, including executed criminals and those accused of witchcraft. This was often referred to as *burial without the sanctuary* or *to lie out of the sanctuary*. Another old saying is that the devil walks in dark places; originally a reference to shadowy areas of a churchyard, especially the north side of a church. Burials were prohibited by the council from taking place on the north side of St. Nicholas' Church until 1648, when the growth of the town's population was causing a lack of burial space. In 1799, the churchyard was enlarged to Factory Road when part of the town wall and a gate east of the Minster were demolished.

Roger Silver

George W. Beech (1901-1979)
Printer, Wood Carver, Craftsmen and Author

Pit Road, Hemsby
Introduced by Andrew Fakes
Unveiled by Councillor Jim Shrimplin
April 2012

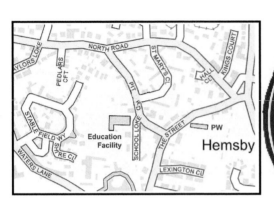

Printer, Wood Carver
& Craftsman

GEORGE W. BEECH
1901 – 1979
LIVED HERE
and Author of a
History of Hemsby

G.Y.L.H.&A.S.

George Beech

George Beech carried on several trades, making fine furniture and beautiful signs, but it was generally agreed that he would only work when 'the fancy took him'. He remained a bachelor all his life, but had many friendships, usually based in public houses. It was also his great pleasure to regale holiday makers with his numerous collections of stories, many of which were 'off colour', but some of them were actually true.

He wrote *The Story of Hemsby-on-Sea* a couple of years before he died, which contained many anecdotes about life in the village. However, not all of his history would stand up to modern scholarship.

He liked to think of himself as a man of the 18th century and worked with hand tools. He would get his timber directly from the tree without modern aids. Indeed, his house was not connected to mains electricity, water supply or sewers. Hence, George's standard of personal cleanliness did not make him universally popular.

He was, however, always referred to as a *Hemsby Character* and an example of a bygone age.

Andrew Fakes

Nobody Famous Lived Here

or ANYTHING really HAPPENED HERE

So this plaque, is probably a waste of time.

Gorleston Sense of Humour Society

Whimsical Walker (Thomas Dawson Walker) (1850-1934)
World Famous Clown

Gorleston Old Cemetery
Introduced by Dusty Miller in the presence of Whimsical Walker's great grandson, Whimmie the clown
Unveiled by the Mayor, Councillor Adrian Thompson
Sponsored by Gorleston-on-Sea Heritage
10th May 2022

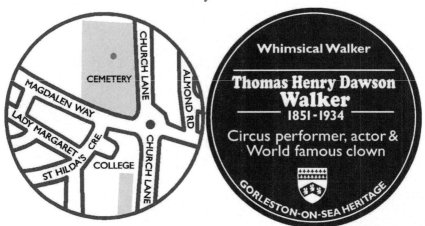

Whimsical Walker, the oldest working clown in the world, died at his home, 42 Suffolk Road, Gorleston in November 1934. A few days earlier he was planning to appear once again at Christmas at the scene of so many of his big triumphs; the Olympia Circus. Walker had been 73 years in the circus business. Two years before his death he underwent a serious operation on his throat. He married his wife in 1910, whom he had met when they were both appearing in a comic sketch in Southend and they lived in Gorleston after the wedding.

Walker was born in Hull in the *March of Intellect*, a public house, kept by his mother, who had married the manager of Cook's Circus. As a child he played such parts as *a living head without a body,* when he showed his head through a trap door with great effect. As a boy he played in a country circus, when admission cost a penny, and he was a link, one of the few surviving, with the heyday of pantomime harlequinade.

At the age of eight years he performed with Pablo Fanque's Circus, where he learnt the business of being a circus performer. When in his teens, he was called upon to play Little Willie in *East Lynn* and the ghost in *Hamlet.* On his second trip to the United States of America in 1879, he travelled by caravan from New York to San Francisco through districts occupied by little else than buffaloes and Red Indians.

Whimsical Walker

In 1874, he was engaged by Charles Hengler to appear at his circus in London, where he was christened *Whimsical Walker*.

Tradition has it that every successful comedian's ambition is to play *Hamlet.* If Walker ever had that urge it was satisfied, for in about 1894, he did take the part at Olympia, though it was in a condensed and humorous version. It was a great success, and he played the part eight times a day for 12 weeks.

Walker appeared before Kings, Queens and Prime Ministers. He clowned his way through continents and visited the United States of America several times. His first visit was in 1874, when he joined the John Murray Railroad Circus and later he toured with Barman and Bailey's Circus. While he was with Barnum's, he purchased an elephant from the London Zoo, which became known as Jumbo. He was in pantomime at the Drury Lane Theatre for 31 years and for 13 years he appeared at the Olympia Circus.

In 1882, Whimsical Walker opened a theatre of his own in New York with a pantomime called *Three Wishes*. Its success brought misfortune, for the top gallery dropped a bit when filled with people and a stampede followed, and actions for damages reduced Walker to the clothes he wore and a few dollars. He had to borrow money to return to Liverpool, where he was engaged by Hengler's Circus.

Whimsical Walker's great grandson, Whimie Walker

Walker has been described as the most versatile clown of his day. He had a great talent for training animals, among them a donkey, which once escaped from a circus procession in Hull and walked into a hotel bedroom and lay down on a bed, thoroughly scaring a chambermaid. One of the animals which he loved most was Whimmy, his dog, who performed with him at Olympia.

Whimsical Walker's unmarked grave

Recalling the occasion when he appeared before Queen Victoria at Windsor in 1886, Walker related: the show took place in the riding school, which the Queen had not entered since the death of Prince Albert. Walker took his singing donkey with him and a German groom. She came to see the donkey and patted his back, whereupon the donkey turned around and let fly with his heels. The Queen said: *take him away, I have had enough of him.* The donkey was taken to the Royal Mews, while the band played *See the Conquering Hero Comes*. However, Queen Victoria presented Walker with a diamond tie pin. In 1934, he was performing when Princess Elizabeth attended her first circus.

King Edward, then the Prince of Wales, once called upon Walker to organise a cricket match with children in which the Prince and Dr. W. G. Grace both joined in.

Walker said that: *the finest thing in the world for any young boy is the circus business: you get fresh air, you get up early in the morning, you get plenty of exercise, and it teaches you what the world is.*

Such was his enthusiasm for his job that he once travelled by sea to Sydney and back, in order to be the clown for five nights and two matinees. Walker was very proud of having had his portrait painted by Dame Laura Knight and which was hung in the Royal Academy. Walker appeared in films including: *The Starting Point* (1919), *The Fordington Twins* (1920) and *The Knut and the Kernel* (1915).

Paul P. Davies

Captain George William Manby FRS (1765-1854)
Barrack Master and Inventor of Marine Lifesaving Equipment

Bauleah House, St. Nicholas Road, Great Yarmouth
Unveiled by the Mayor, Councillor Graham Plant
17th July 2022

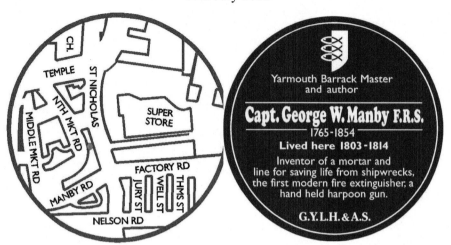

George Manby

Manby was born at Hilgay near Downham Market in Norfolk in 1765. He entered the Military Academy, Woolwich in 1776. When his parents died, Manby returned to Hilgay to manage the family estate. He combined estate working with soldiering by entering the Cambridgeshire Militia. With the outbreak of the war with France the regiment was moved to Warley in Essex. His Captain there was the Honourable Charles Yorke who later became the Secretary-at-War.

Manby married Jane Preston of Waldingfield. Her lavish lifestyle nearly bankrupted him and, in 1797, he was forced to sell his estate. Later his wife eloped with an officer of the East India Company. In a subsequent duel with the officer in 1799, Manby survived being shot in the head. Manby wrote: *the slugs that were deeply imbedded in my head were taken out. It was one of the most painful operations that, perhaps, ever a mortal underwent. On my death, I have directed that my head be taken off, and with the bullets, delivered to Yarmouth born surgeon, Sir Astley Cooper, trusting that some public benefit may result. The person who performed the operation assured me that a trepanning was necessary and that he distinctly saw my brain.* His first wife, Jane, died in 1814 and in 1818 he married Sophie, the daughter of Sir Thomas Gooch of Benacre Hall in Suffolk.

In about 1802, Manby settled at Clifton near Bristol. During this time he wrote *The History and Antiquities of St David's, Sketches of the History and Natural Beauties of Clifton and A Guide from Clifton to the Counties of Monmouth, Glamorgan* etc. All these books were illustrated with his own drawings. Later he wrote about the threatened invasion of England by Napoleon.

This last work attracted the attention of Charles Yorke, now the Secretary-at-War. In August 1803, Yorke appointed Manby as Barrack Master at Great Yarmouth. Manby had previously

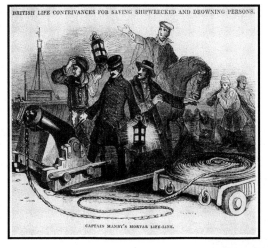

BRITISH LIFE CONTRIVANCES FOR SAVING SHIPWRECKED AND DROWNING PERSONS.

CAPTAIN MANBY'S MORTAR LIFE-LINE.

offered his services to Yorke to assassinate Napoleon. He moved to the Cottage on the Denes (now Bauleah House) at the north end of, what is now, Manby Road.

When the old barracks, of which he was the master, in St. Nicholas' Road was sold by the Government in 1814, Manby became the Barrack Master at the Royal Naval Hospital/Barracks at Great Yarmouth, with the rank of captain-lieutenant.

Manby invented an apparatus for saving the lives of shipwrecked sailors marooned on their vessels. A 6lb. mortar was used to carry a rope from the shore to the stricken vessel. His first idea was to use the line fired from the mortar to pull a boat to the shipwreck. This was adapted later to use a sling to bring sailors ashore. His greatest difficulty was to create a fireproof link between the shot and the line. Chain and rope broke under the sudden strain of the shot and eventually he successfully used plaited hide. With the mortar he could fire a line 400 yards. During his lifetime 1,000 sailors were rescued using his apparatus. His interest in saving lives from shipwrecks developed after watching the loss, in a

The Snipe gun brig aground at Yarmouth in 1807
Painting by Francis Sarto

gale, of the gun brig *Snipe*, off Yarmouth in 1807 when 67 people drowned within 60 yards of the shore. The *Snipe* was carrying 30 French prisoners of war, a full crew and some women. During this severe north northeasterly gale twelve ships were wrecked on the shore between Cromer and Yarmouth.

Later in his life he invented the hand-held harpoon gun, which he tested on a voyage to the Arctic. He wrote about the voyage in 1822 in an article entitled *Journal of a Voyage to Greenland*.

Manby was elected a Fellow of the Royal Society in 1831.

He moved to Southtown in 1842. The only monument to him was the one he erected in his front garden. Manby also invented a portable fire extinguisher and a lifeboat.

Manby died, penniless, at his house in Southtown, Great Yarmouth in 1854, at the age of 88 years. He had built up a collection of the relics of Nelson in this house. He was buried close to his mother and father in Hilgay churchyard.

A rescue using Manby's line

Paul P. Davies

Anne Pashley (1935 -2016)
Athlete, Olympic Medalist and Operatic Soprano

Marine Lodge, 19-20 Euston Road, Great Yarmouth
Unveiled by the Mayor, Councillor Graham Plant
17th July 2022

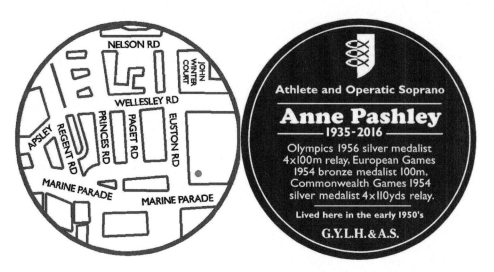

Anne Pashley was a British sprinter and following her athletic career, she became an operatic soprano.

She was born in Skegness, Lincolnshire, the younger of two daughters of Roy Pashley, an English teacher, and his wife Milly Pashley, who ran a holiday camp. Anne was very young when the family moved to Stroud, Gloucester, for her father's work. However, her asthma meant that when she was 14 years of age the family were advised to relocate to the coast and they ended up in Great Yarmouth. It was while she was studying at Great Yarmouth High School for Girls that her running potential was first spotted. In January 1954, her parents purchased Hill's Marine View Hotel (now Marine Lodge) with 47 bedrooms for £10,000. It had been out of commission for 14 years, after it was damaged during the war.

After joining Great Yarmouth Athletics Club, Pashley soon began competing in county championships and representing her country. In 1953, at the Amateur Athletic Association championships in White City, Pashley equalled the British women's 100 yards record of 10.8 seconds. She took bronze in the 100 metres at the 1954 European Athletics Championships in Bern, Switzerland. Also, in 1954, she took silver in the 4 x 110 yards relay at the British Empire and Commonwealth Games in Vancouver.

Anne Pashley

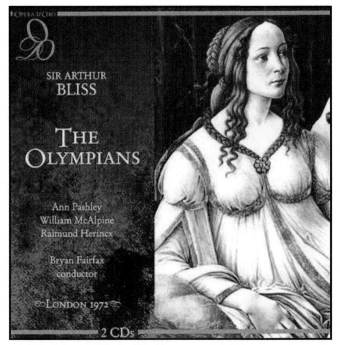

In 1956, she was one of nine female athletes chosen to represent Great Britain at the Olympics in Melbourne in the women's 100 metres and the 4x100 metres relay. While she failed to qualify for the 100 metres final, Pashley, along with Jean Scrivens, June Foulds and Heather Armitage took silver behind the Australians in the relay.

Pashley retired from athletic competition soon after the Melbourne Olympics and went on to become a star of the Royal Opera House. In 1959, having trained at the Guildhall School of Music, London, Pashley made her debut in the Handel Opera Society's production of *Semele* at Sadler's Wells Theatre.

She spent the next 30 years performing as a soprano at some of the world's most renowned opera houses including Glyndebourne, the Royal Opera at Covent Garden and across Europe, as well as securing the leading roles in eight BBC TV operas and numerous radio broadcasts. She also sang for Welsh National Opera, Scottish Opera, Kent Opera and the New Opera Company.

She died in 2016 after suffering with bone cancer.

Her voice can be heard on youtube: www.youtube.com/watch?v=y5NBSAcgtVQ

Paul P. Davies

Pashley, second from left, winning a silver medal at the 1956 Olympics

Sir William Gooch (1681-1751) First Baronet
Soldier and the Governor of Virginia from 1727 to 1749

7-8 South Quay, Great Yarmouth
August 2022

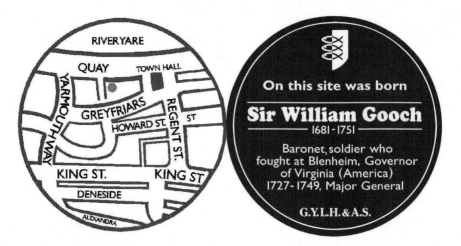

William Gooch

One of the great losses in St. Nicholas' Church following the 1942 incendiary bombing during the Second World War, were the memorials. In 1840, we are told that there were 500 memorials and gravestones inside the church. Wandering around before the Second World War, one would have been reminded of the history of Great Yarmouth and the important people, who once lived here. One such person was Sir William Gooch, who was born in a house at the north-west corner of Queen Street, Great Yarmouth and who had a splendid memorial in the church. By the age of 15 years, both parents had died and his elder brother, Thomas, supervised his education. Thomas became successively Bishop of Bristol, Norwich, and Ely.

William Gooch had planned to enter Oxford University, but instead purchased a commission in the Army. In 1727, through Gooch's connections with the politically powerful the Duke of Newcastle, King George I appointed him Governor of Virginia and he served there until 1749. He was one of Virginia's ablest and most successful chief executives. One of his greatest success was the passage of the Tobacco Inspection Act of 1730, which called for the inspection and regulation of Virginia's tobacco; its most important crop. Tobacco planters were required to transport their crop to public warehouses, where it was inspected and stored. The Act raised the quality of Virginia's tobacco and reduced fraud and this greatly increased the demand for its tobacco in Europe.

Gooch's military policy focused on protecting the western territory from native Indian and French encroachment. Western expansion was fraught by repeated Indian invasions. Gooch decided to broker peace to end the warfare. His resignation, because of failing health, was profoundly regretted by the Virginians and he returned to England in 1749.

Gooch named part of the colony, Goochland County (population in 2020 was 24,727 and has an area of 290 square miles).

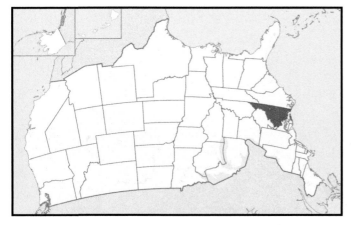

Virginia, America

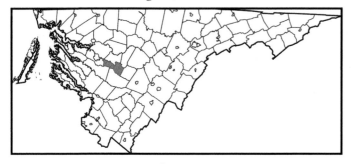

Goochland, Virginia

Gooch had an interesting military career. He fought under John Churchill, the 1st Duke of Marlborough in the Low Countries, including the important victory at the Battle of Blenheim (1704). In 1715, he served with the English, who repelled the Jacobite uprising in Scotland. Gooch served in the expedition against Cartagena, now in Columbia in South America, as part of the War of Jenkins' Ear. Gooch was wounded in both ankles by a cannon ball in the attack in 1740, which left him a cripple. He subsequently suffered poor health for the rest of his life, probably due to malaria.

In about 1744, Gooch declined the appointment of being in charge of the army raised to invade Canada.

Gooch was created a baronet in 1746 and a Major General in 1747. He was a staunch member of the Church of England and condemned all religious groups apart from the established church. He focused on what he perceived as threats from new Protestant denominations such as the Methodists and the Baptists. However, in 1738, Gooch had given a group of Presbyterians the right to settle new territory in America.

He visited Bath several times in the hope of improving his health, but without success. Gooch died in 1751 and was buried in St. Nicholas' Church in his native town of Great Yarmouth, where his widow erected an elaborate funerary monument in white marble on the wall of the north aisle. This displayed the highlights of his career. A residence hall at the College of William and Mary in Williamsburg, Virginia is named in his honour

Paul P. Davies

.

Printed in Great Britain
by Amazon